Microwave Cooking Made Easy

GW00691261

Douglas Marsland

Bay Books / Sydney & London

Contents

Introduction 4

This revised edition published by
Bay Books
61-69 Anzac Parade
Kensington NSW 2033

© Text and Illustrations Bay Books

Publisher: George Barber

National Library of Australia Card Number
and ISBN 0 85835 338 5

Photographer: Norman Nicholls
Front cover photograph by Ashley Barber
Printed in Singapore
by TOPPAN PRINTING CO.

BBR1287

Introduction

Microwave ovens are rapidly revolutionising our kitchens. It will only be a matter of time before one is found in every home. Microwave cooking is fast, efficient, clean, cool and economical. The only heat is within the food itself, therefore the oven and kitchen remain cool. This is a marvellous feature when the oven is used in small apartments, mobile homes and caravans. The oven can also be used for outdoor entertaining or beside a pool — wherever a powerpoint is available. To clean the oven, simply wipe out with a damp cloth.

Microwave ovens can be used to prepare every meal (breakfasts, quick luncheons or formal dinners) with menus ranging from appetisers to soups, entrées, main courses and desserts. Coffee can also be percolated in a Pyrex jug. The cost of operating the oven is still under ten cents per hour.

RECENT TECHNOLOGICAL CHANGES

The first microwave ovens that were introduced for home use in 1967 had only basic features. The oven had only one power level, requiring the cooking times to be varied to achieve the desired results.

Since then there have been a number of major improvements: **automatic defrosting** (which allows for even and thorough defrosting — eliminating the need to turn the oven on and off by hand); **variable power temperature control** (providing a range of cooking temperatures, and making it possible to cook an endless variety of food); **sensor probe** (a device which, when inserted into large pieces of meat or poultry, controls the cooking of the food to a desired internal temperature rather than to a set time — allowing for 'rare', 'medium' and 'well-done' selections); **combination ovens** (which use convection cooking — either gas or electric — with microwave cooking to start or finish the dish).

Other new oven features include cooking and defrosting by weight, computer memory and delay-stand. These combinations enable food to be cooked in a preset oven if you should be away from your home. The food can then be held at the required temperature on the warm variable until required. Microwave ovens are also available with a browning grill within the oven, which can be lowered to enable food to be grilled and browned to your liking.

Today we can choose from 500, 600 and 650 watt models, with a range of cabinet sizes to suit even the smallest kitchen.

ADVANTAGES OF THE MICROWAVE OVEN

- Cooking time is extremely short.
- Food is not burnt.
- Microwave ovens can cook food contained in glass, china, or wrapped in plastic film.
- Food does not lose its original shape, flavour and nutrient value.
- Germs are killed.
- Operating costs are much lower than for a conventional oven as preheating is not necessary.
- Microwave ovens do not generate heat; all the energy produced is absorbed by the food in the oven, and the kitchen temperature remains comfortable.

WHAT IS A MICROWAVE?

A microwave is an electromagnetic wave within a particular frequency band. It is similar to electromagnetic waves found in radio, light and heatwaves. A microwave is generated by electricity passing through a special vacuum tube called a magnetron.

Microwaves operate on a communications frequency band and, because of this, they are regulated by the Federal Communications Commission. This regulatory body has designated two frequencies for uses other than communications; one is 915 megahertz, and the other is 2450 megahertz.

To fully understand why a microwave causes food to cook, you need to know how unique it is. A microwave produced at 2450 megahertz is about 11 centimetres in length. These waves travel in straight lines, but can be reflected, transmitted and absorbed. It is these special qualities of a microwave which enable us to generate heat and use it as a cooking source. The resulting appliance is a microwave oven.

WHAT IS A MICROWAVE OVEN?

The design of a microwave oven is very important in that each of its parts is directly related to the generation and direction of microwaves to food.

The basic oven has the following parts: power cord, transformer, magnetron tube, wave guide, stirrer, oven cavity, glass shelf, and door.

Power Cord

An appliance cord which supplies the electricity to the oven.

Transformer

Increases incoming voltage to the high voltage necessary to produce microwaves at 2450 megahertz.

Magnetron Tube

A vacuum tube which converts electrical energy into microwaves.

Wave Guide

A rectangular metal tube whose function is to distribute microwaves into the oven cavity.

Stirrer

A slowly moving metal fan which agitates the microwaves evenly in the oven cavity. An important factor in obtaining a good cooking pattern of microwaves within the oven.

Oven Cavity

A metal box with an acrylic interior surface, which retains the microwaves and continually directs them to the food.

Glass Shelf

Elevates the cooking utensils off the bottom of the oven to allow the metal bottom of the oven to redirect the microwaves back to the centre of the oven.

Door

A see-through door with a punched metal screen which permits viewing the inside of the oven, but also reflects the microwaves back into the oven.

HOW A MICROWAVE OVEN WORKS

The microwave oven uses microwaves of 2450 megahertz (2450 000 000 cycles or vibrations per second). When microwave energy comes in contact with a substance, any one or a combination of three things may occur:

- it can be reflected;
- it can be transmitted;
- it can be absorbed.

When it is absorbed the energy is converted into heat. Cooking with microwave energy differs from conventional cooking in that there is no direct application of heat to food. In traditional cooking, heat energy is absorbed by the food; this is a slow process. As microwaves pass through to the food in the oven, they cause the water molecules within the food to vibrate at extremely high speeds. This friction produces the intense heat which cooks the food. Microwave energy is odourless and tasteless, so it cannot affect the flavour of the food you cook. Food cooked by microwaves will usually taste better than food cooked conventionally and, as microwave cooking is more rapid, fewer vitamins and flavours are lost.

COOKING UTENSILS — DISHES YOU MAY USE

Chinaware

China dishes without metal trim.

Paper Products

Paper plates, cups, napkins and paper towels may be used in the oven, but only for a few minutes. They are not suitable for use in cooking.

Plastic Containers

Most plastics can be used for warming foods, but again, only for a few minutes. They are not suitable for use in cooking.

Straw and Wood

Use only for heating foods — a few minutes only.

Heat-resistant Glass

Heat-proof glass utensils that are labelled bakeware, ovenware or ovenproof are excellent.

Cooking Bags

These bags are ideal for using in the microwave oven. Use a string tie instead of the small metal tie. Pierce a hole in the bag for steam to escape.

DISH TEST

The following test will help you to determine whether your dishes are suitable for use in a microwave oven.

- Place a china or heat-resistant glass cup filled with water in the dish to be tested.
- Place both of them in the microwave oven.
- Set the timer for 1½ minutes.
- If the water is very warm and the dish cool, you may use the dish. If the water is cool and the dish is warm or hot, do not use the dish.

COOKWARE YOU SHOULD NOT USE

Do not use metal pans, or dishes with a metal trim. Microwaves are reflected by metal, and so this will cause arcing that could damage your oven. Do not use foil pans, aluminium foil, or cups with glued handles.

Remember: Using metal inside your microwave oven can shorten the life of the magnetron tube!

THINGS YOU SHOULD NOT DO

- Do not operate the microwave oven when it is empty. When there is no food to absorb it, microwave energy can damage the magnetron tube.
- Do not use metal cookware of any kind in the oven. The use of metal cookware, trays or foil will increase cooking time and decrease energy efficiency. It causes uneven cooking and, as described above, can damage the magnetron tube.
- Do not operate the oven when the door gasket is damaged or dirty. To do so would allow microwave energy to escape. If the gasket becomes worn or damaged, it must be replaced with the special type supplied by the manufacturer.
- Do not allow anyone except an authorised serviceman to service your microwave oven.
- Do not use a regular meat thermometer in the oven while operating. Most meat thermometers contain metal. Special meat thermometers are available for use in microwave ovens.

- Do not rest food or cookware on the door. This can misalign the door and damage the door seal.
- Do not reheat liquids in a microwave oven without first stirring or pouring them. Before heating, mix air into the liquid or break up the surface film (such as forms on soups) to prevent pressure build-up and eruption.
- Do not bake potatoes, tomatoes or apples unless the skins have been pierced. Be sure that all foods with an outer skin or membrane are pierced to allow steam to escape during cooking.
- Similarly, do not cook vegetables in a plastic bag or airtight container unless the bag or container has been pierced.
- Do not cook using a container with a restricted opening, such as a cordial or salad oil bottle.

COOKING ADVICE

Standing Time

Standing time is a fuel-saving bonus, as it allows food to complete cooking even after being removed from the oven. Standing time allows the heat to move inward, cooking the centre of the food by conduction. In the case of small items of food, standing time is usually completed in a matter of a minute. Large items of food such as poultry or roasts of meat, require 15-20 minutes — or half the cooking time. After removal from the oven, these large items should be wrapped in foil to retain the heat. During this time the internal temperature will increase by 8-10°C, thus completing the cooking cycle. During this time vegetables and sauces can be cooked.

Using the Recipes in this Book

The times listed for each recipe represent the **total** cooking time required for all the preparation stages of that dish.

Weights and Measures

Fluid measures are given in millilitres and litres; solid measures are given in grams and kilograms.
The following conversion equivalents may be of use:

    One cup = 250 ml
    4 cups = 1 litre
    1 teaspoon = 5 ml
Note that all measurements should be level.

Recipe conversion

To convert your favourite recipes for microwave cooking, allow one-quarter of the conventional cooking time. The actual cooking time will not, in fact be less — it could be more. If this should be the case, cook 2 to 3 minutes longer and allow for standing time. It is always best to undercook unless you are not sure of the exact cooking time. Over-cooking cannot be corrected. Liquids should also be reduced. If a recipe for a conventional oven calls for one cup of liquid, reduce it to three-quarters of a cup. Seasonings should also be reduced until the cooking is completed.

VARIABLE POWER LEVELS IN MICROWAVE OVENS

HIGH	100%	For vegetables, fish, meat and beverages. Use pre-heat browning grill.
SAUTÉ	90%	For onions, celery, capsicum and quick-cooking foods.
REHEAT	80%	For reheating food.
ROAST	70%	(medium high) For roasts, meat loaves, and ham.
BAKE	60%	For cakes and bread.
SIMMER	50%	(medium) For soups and stews.
BRAISE	40%	(slow cook) For tough cuts of meat.
DEFROST	30%	For defrosting food, making lemon butter and some cheese cakes.
LOW	20%	For small amounts of food that must be cooked slowly.
WARM	10%	For keeping food warm and softening butter; for cream cheese, chocolate and frozen bread dough.

WATTAGE
Recipes included in this book were cooked in a 500 watt oven. If you are using a 600, 650 or 700 watt oven, reduce cooking time by approximately 10 per cent.

DEFROSTING FROZEN FOODS ON THE DEFROST CYCLE

SEAFOOD	Weight	Defrosting Time in Minutes
Fish fillets—As fillets defrost, remove them from the frozen portion to prevent them from cooking.	500 g	10-12
Whole fish	750 g	12-14
Cooked prawns	500 g	5-6
Mud crabs	500-750 g	12-14
Lobster tails	250 g	7
Scallops	500 g	5-6

POULTRY		
Poultry may be defrosted in its original plastic wrap. Remove metal clip to prevent arcing. Place in glass dish to catch defrosted liquid.		
Whole chicken	1-1.5 kg	20
Chicken pieces (drumsticks, wings and thighs)	500 g	8
Whole chicken breasts	250 g	6-8
Chicken Livers	500 g	8
Turkey Defrost on the *Roast cycle* This size of turkey would take approximately 1 hour on the *Defrost cycle*.	4-6 kg	Cook 15 minutes. Rest 10 minutes. Turn over. Repeat cooking. Place into cold water to complete defrosting.
Ducks Defrost on the *Roast cycle* On the *Defrost cycle* this size of duck would take approximately 35 minutes.	2-2.5 kg	Cook 10 minutes. Rest 10 minutes. Turn over. Repeat. Complete defrosting in cold water.

MEAT

Thaw meat in original wrapping.

	Weight	Defrosting Time in Minutes	Standing Time at Room Temperature in Minutes
Rolled roast	2 kg	35	60
Rump roast	2 kg	25	60
Lamb leg of	2 kg	30	60
Corned beef	1-1.5 kg	15	30
Pork leg	2-2.5 kg	30-45	60
Whole fillet of beef	2.5 kg	10-15	10
Sliced steak	1.5 kg	10-15	5
Minced steak	500 g	9	5
Pork spareribs	1-1.5 kg	20	5
Pork and lamb chops	1 kg	15	10
Veal steak schnitzel	500 g	7	5

Breakfast and Accompaniments

Sausage, Bacon and Eggs

Many recipe books suggest that eggs cannot be cooked in their shells in a microwave oven, but this is not true.
Just follow the directions given and the eggs will not explode.

Eggs require careful handling when cooked in a microwave oven. Egg yolks and whites cook at different speeds, so both the whites and the yolks must be pierced with a toothpick before frying.

Overcooking will give you a rubbery, tough egg, so remove your eggs or egg dishes from the oven just before they are fully cooked.
Allow them to stand outside the oven for a few minutes and they will finish cooking on their own.

When a particular dish calls for a cheese topping, remember to add it at the end of the cooking period as cheese quickly becomes tough and rubbery.

OATMEAL FOR 1 TIME: 1½ MINUTES (HIGH)

¼ cup quick cooking oats
⅛ teaspoon salt
½ cup water, at room temperature

Place oatmeal, water and salt into a serving bowl. Cook 1 minute 30 seconds, stir, cover, and let stand for a few minutes before serving.
Note: May be cooked in advance and reheated.

GRILLED GRAPEFRUIT FOR 2 TIME: 2 MINUTES (HIGH)

1 grapefruit
2 teaspoons brown sugar
2 teaspoons sherry

Cut grapefruit in half and segment. Place onto a plate and sprinkle with brown sugar and sherry. Cook 1½-2 minutes for 2 halves.

BOILED EGG TIME: 3½ MINUTES (DEFROST)

1 55 g egg at room temperature
1 teaspoon salt
water to cover egg

Boil water in small jug or bowl. Add 1 teaspoon salt, then the egg. Cook on *Defrost Cycle* for 3½-4 minutes.

SCRAMBLED EGGS FOR 2 TIME: 4 MINUTES (HIGH)

4 55 g eggs at room temperature
¼ cup milk or cream
½ teaspoon salt
1½ tablespoons butter

Combine eggs, milk, salt, in a bowl. Melt butter in a glass bowl for 30 seconds. Pour in egg mixture and cover with plastic food wrap. Cook 2 minutes, stir well and cook another 1½ minutes stirring 2 or 3 times. Remove eggs when softer than required and let stand for 1 minute.

WITH CHEESE
Add 1 tablespoon grated cheese to beaten eggs and milk. Add a few seconds to total cooking time.

WITH BACON AND CHIVES
Chop 1-2 rashers of bacon, cook 1-2 minutes. Cook eggs 1 minute, add bacon with 2 teaspoons chopped chives, stir well, continue cooking.

FRIED EGG TIME: 55 SECONDS (HIGH)

1 55 g egg at room temperature
½ teaspoon butter

Melt butter on a plate for 25 seconds. Add egg, prick yolk 2-3 times with a toothpick. Cook 30 seconds.

Note:
2 eggs — 1 minute 5 seconds.
3 eggs — 1 minute 35 seconds.
4 eggs — 2 minutes.

SAVOURY SCONE RING TIME: 7 MINUTES (HIGH)

2 tablespoons butter
2 tablespoons sugar
1 cup pumpkin, mashed
1 small onion finely cut
2 tablespoons parsley, chopped
1 egg
½ cup milk
2½ cups self-raising flour
½ teaspoon salt

Cream butter and sugar. Add pumpkin, onion and parsley. Add well-beaten egg. Add milk slowly. Cut in sifted flour and salt. Place into a well-greased microwave baking ring. Cook 7-8 minutes, remove and let stand for 4 minutes.

POACHED EGGS TIME: 3½ MINUTES (DEFROST)

2 55 g eggs at room temperature
2 cups water

Boil 2 cups of water in a bowl. Add eggs and cook, covered, on the *Defrost Cycle* 3½-4 minutes.

GRILLS

SAUSAGES:

Heat browning dish for 8 minutes on high. Lightly grease dish. Place up to 6 sausages in the dish and cook 3 minutes on each side on high.
Note: Prick sausages well before grilling and allow 2-3 minutes standing time.

BACON:

Place bacon on several layers of white kitchen paper on a flat dish with one layer of paper covering the bacon. Cook bacon for about 1 minute per slice on high.

SLICED TOMATOES:

Heat browning dish for 6 minutes on high. Grease lightly with butter. Add 9 thick slices of tomato. Coat with buttered herbed crumbs. Cook 1 minute, turn slices and cook another 1-1½ minutes on high.
Note: Use 3 tomatoes cut into 3 thick slices each, cutting off top and bottom so that slices lie flat.

PINEAPPLE AND BANANAS:

Heat browning dish 5 minutes, lightly butter slices of fresh pineapple and cook 4 minutes on one side and 1-1½ minutes on the other. Reheat browning dish as above; using 3 bananas split lengthwise, cook 1-1¼ minutes on one side only.

BACON AND PINEAPPLE SATAY:

Remove rind from thin strip of bacon. Cut into 3 or 4 pieces. Roll up and place onto bamboo satay stick. Place wedge of pineapple between bacon curls. Cook 3-4 minutes between white kitchen paper on high.
Note: Button mushrooms or cherry tomatoes could be used instead of pineapple wedges.

WHOLE MUSHROOMS WITH FRENCH OR GARLIC DRESSING TIME: 2 MINUTES (HIGH)

6 medium mushrooms
French dressing or garlic dressing

Arrange mushrooms in a circle on a plate and sprinkle each with ½ teaspoon of your favourite dressing and cook, covered, for 2 minutes.

SLICED MUSHROOMS TIME: 2 MINUTES (HIGH)

250 g mushrooms, thinly sliced
1 tablespoon lemon juice
1 tablespoon parsley, chopped
60 g butter

Arrange mushrooms in a shallow dish. Sprinkle with lemon juice and parsley. Dot with butter and cook covered for 2 minutes on high.

STUFFED MUSHROOMS TIME: 3 MINUTES (HIGH)

6 medium mushrooms, whole
2 slices ham
125 g cream cheese
1 tablespoon chives

Remove stalks from mushrooms. Chop ham finely and combine with cheese and chives. Spread mixture into cavity of mushrooms and cook, covered, 3 minutes on high.

TEA, COFFEE OR CUPS OF SOUP

Fill cups or coffee mugs with cold water. Heat uncovered in the oven on high.
1 cup—approximately 2½ minutes, depending on size of cup.
2 cups—approximately 4½ minutes.
Then add your instant coffee, tea bag, or your single serving of instant soup mix.

Note: Milk may be heated for coffee or tea, also for oatmeal.

GOLDEN CORN BREAD TIME: 7 MINUTES (HIGH)

2 tablespoons butter or vegetable oil
2 tablespoons sugar
1½ cups plain flour
4 teaspoons baking powder
1 cup cornmeal
¼ teaspoon salt
¼ teaspoon chilli powder
2 eggs, beaten
¾ cup milk
125 g cream style corn
¼ cup red capsicum, diced

Cream butter and sugar. Add sifted flour and baking powder. Add cornmeal, salt and chilli powder. Stir in eggs, milk and beat until smooth. Fold in corn and capsicum. Place into a well-greased microwave baking ring and cook 7-8 minutes on high. Remove and let stand 4 minutes.

SCONES TIME: 10 MINUTES (HIGH)

2 cups self raising flour
1 tablespoon sugar
½ teaspoon salt
1½ tablespoons milk butter
¾ cup milk

Sift flour into basin, add sugar and salt. Cut butter into small cubes, rub into flour. Add milk, blend mixture with a tableknife. Turn onto floured board. Cut into rounds. Heat browning dish 8 minutes — on high. Cook scones 1 minute on each side on high. 8 scones.

CHIVE & HAM SCONES
add 1 tablespoon cut chives
1 tablespoon diced ham to mixture
Delete sugar

Soups and Snacks

Bread Cases

Individual portions of soup in mugs heat best in a microwave oven. When preparing bigger quantities use a large casserole and stir frequently to distribute the heat evenly. A wooden spoon can be left in the casserole for stirring while the soup is cooking.

A microwave oven is very handy for preparing snacks. For a party, for example, snacks and appetisers can be made in advance, frozen, and reheated when needed.

Appetisers can be heated on their serving plates, which makes it even easier.

BREAD CASES

TIME: 4 MINUTES (HIGH)

6 thin slices of brown or white bread
butter
1 micromuffin pan

FILLING SUGGESTIONS:
1 cup cheese sauce and add **either**
1 cup of cream style corn
1 cup flaked salmon
1 cup assorted seafood (prawns,
  crabmeat, oysters)
1 cup chopped green asparagus

Remove crusts from bread. Place bread in oven and cook 1 minute to refresh. Butter bread. Place butter side down into muffin pan, so that the corners form four peaks. Place into oven and cook 2-3 minutes. Remove cases, which should be firm and crisp.

MACARONI AND CHEESE

TIME: 18 MINUTES (HIGH)   SERVES 4

1 cup macaroni, uncooked
1 litre hot water
½ teaspoon salt

2 cups cheese, grated
2 eggs
1 milk
½ teaspoon prepared mustard
dash of salt
dash of paprika
dash of Worcestershire sauce

Place macaroni into a 2 litre casserole with water and salt. Cook in oven 10 minutes on high or until macaroni is tender. Stir after 5 minutes. Drain, rinse in hot water.

Place a layer of macaroni in a baking dish and sprinkle with grated cheese. Repeat, alternating macaroni and cheese, ending with cheese. Beat eggs lightly in a bowl. Add milk, mustard, salt and Worcestershire sauce. Stir well. Drizzle mixture on macaroni. Sprinkle with paprika. Cook, covered, 8 minutes, stirring after 4 minutes.

TUNA-STUFFED CAPSICUMS

TIME: 18 MINUTES (HIGH)   SERVES 4

4-6 large capsicums
500 g canned tuna
1 cup soft breadcrumbs
½ cup celery, finely diced
⅓ cup mayonnaise
1 egg
2 tablespoons lemon juice
2 tablespoons prepared mustard
2 tablespoons soft butter
1 tablespoon onion, finely chopped
¼ teaspoon salt
⅛ teaspoon tabasco sauce
2 slices cheese

Cut a slice from the upper third of each capsicum. Dice strips that have been cut off. Remove seeds and membrane from inside of capsicum. Parboil capsicum in oven for 5 minutes. Drain. Mix diced capsicum with remaining ingredients. Fill capsicums and stand them in a casserole dish. Cook covered on high 12 minutes.

Top with cheese strips in form of cross. Cook 1 minute on high.

Tuna Stuffed Capsicums

CRAB AND SWEET CORN SOUP

TIME: 20 MINUTES (HIGH)	SERVES 6

6 cups chicken stock
1 cup crabmeat
1 cup cream style corn
1 tablespoon cornflour, water
1 tablespoon sherry (dry)
½ teaspoon salt
½ teaspoon oil
½ teaspoon sesame oil
2 eggs, beaten
½ cup shallots, finely chopped

Place stock into a large casserole dish and cook for 15 minutes or until boiling on high. Add crabmeat and corn and cook a further 2 minutes. Add blended cornflour, sherry, salt and oils and bring to the boil, approximately 3 minutes. Remove from oven and add egg slowly to form egg flower. Add shallots. Serve hot.

QUICHE LORRAINE

PASTRY TIME: 6 MINUTES	SERVES 4-6

1¼ cups plain flour
¼ teaspoon baking powder
pinch of salt
⅓ cup margarine
2 tablespoons water
squeeze of lemon juice
1 egg yolk

Sift dry ingredients into a bowl. Rub in margarine using fingertips until mixture resembles fine breadcrumbs. Combine remaining ingredients. Make a well in the centre of dry ingredients, gradually add liquid, mixing to form a dry dough. Turn onto a lightly floured surface, roll out to fit a deep 23 cm glass pie plate. Cook 6 minutes.

FILLING TIME: 12 MINUTES (MEDIUM)
3 eggs
1 cup cream
1 cup milk
pinch of nutmeg, sugar, cayenne pepper
  and white pepper
4 rashers bacon, chopped
1 cup tasty cheese, grated

Whisk eggs, cream, milk, and spices in a mixing bowl. Lightly fry bacon. Sprinkle bacon and cheese over cooked pastry shell. Pour liquid mixture carefully into pastry shell. Cook, uncovered in microwave oven for 12 minutes on medium. Allow to stand 5 minutes before serving. Garnish with parsley and serve.

SEAFOOD CREPES

TIME: 5 MINUTES (MEDIUM)	SERVES 6

CREPES
60 g plain flour
150 ml milk
salt and pepper
parsley, finely chopped
1 egg
15 g butter, melted
30 g lard, to grease crepe pan

Mix all ingredients except lard to make a batter. Grease crepe pan with lard. Heat on range top. Add 1½-2 tablespoons of mixture. Cook until mixture bubbles, turn over and cook a further minute until lightly brown.

FILLING
125 g cooked crabmeat, frozen or canned
125 g cooked prawns
125 g cooked scallops
2 cups cheese sauce (see sauce section)
2 tablespoons chives, finely cut
1-2 tablespoons parsley, finely cut

Combine all ingredients. Place 2 tablespoons mixture onto each crepe. Roll up and place side by side into a casserole dish and cook for 5 minutes on medium. Serve with lemon wedges.

LASAGNA WITH TOPSIDE MINCE

TIME: 48 MINUTES (HIGH)	SERVES 6

250 g lasagna noodles
8 cups boiling water
1 tablespoon salt
1 tablespoon oil
1 tablespoon butter, softened
1 cup onion, sliced
¼ cup mushrooms, sliced
500 g topside mince
1 clove garlic, chopped
1 (250 g) can tomato puree
1 (180 g) can tomato paste
1½ cups beef stock
½ teaspoon sugar
½ teaspoon salt
dash of pepper
1 teaspoon basil
500 g cottage cheese
250 g mozzarella cheese slices
½ cup parmesan cheese, grated

Place lasagna noodles in a casserole. Pour over boiling water. Add salt. Cook 16 minutes on high until tender. Drain and mix with a little oil. Set aside. Melt butter in casserole 30 seconds. Sauté onion in butter 3 minutes. Add mushrooms. Cook 3 minutes. Remove from casserole. Cook topside mince and garlic in casserole 6 minutes, stirring every 2 minutes. Add onion and mushroom mixture, tomato puree, tomato paste, stock, sugar, salt, pepper and basil. Stir well. Cook, covered, 10 minutes, stirring every 3 minutes to make meat sauce. Layer meat sauce, noodles, cottage cheese and mozzarella cheese in a deep casserole dish. Repeat layers 3 times, ending with meat sauce. Sprinkle parmesan cheese on top. Cook 10 minutes.

MOUSSAKA

TIME: 30 MINUTES (HIGH)	SERVES 6

3 eggplants
4 tablespoons olive oil
500 g minced beef
1 small tin tomato paste
salt, cayenne and oregano
2 medium onions, sliced
1 egg
1 cup sour cream
1½ cups buttered breadcrumbs
tomato for garnish
parsley

Cut unpeeled eggplant into 1 cm slices. Sprinkle with salt and leave to stand for 30 minutes. Drain off liquid. Heat browning skillet 8 minutes, add oil and heat a further 3 minutes. Cook eggplant on each side 2 minutes. Combine meat, tomato paste and seasonings. Place layers of eggplant, meat mixture and sliced onion in a greased casserole. Combine beaten egg with sour cream. Spread over mixture. Sprinkle thickly with buttered crumbs and cook 15 minutes on high. Serve hot garnished with tomato and parsley.

CLAM CHOWDER

TIME: 20 MINUTES (HIGH)	SERVES 6

3 rashers of bacon, without rind, diced 1 cm
¼ cup onion, finely chopped
¼ cup celery, finely chopped
¼ cup carrot, finely chopped
¼ cup potato, peeled and diced, 1 cm
3 tablespoons plain flour
1 cup clam juice
2¾ cups milk
1 can clams (250 g)
½ teaspoon thyme
1 bay leaf
1 teaspoon salt
½ teaspoon pepper
¼ cup cream
1 tablespoon parsley, finely chopped

Sprinkle bacon into 2-litre casserole dish, cook 2 minutes. Add vegetables and cook 1 minute. Blend in flour, add clam juice and milk, stir to blend. Add clams and cook 5 minutes. Add thyme, bay leaf, salt and pepper. Cook 12 minutes, stirring after every 3 minutes. Let stand covered for 5 minutes. Remove bay leaf, stir in cream, correct seasoning, sprinkle with parsley and serve.

CABBAGE ROLLS

TIME: 28 MINUTES (HIGH)	SERVES 6

12 cabbage leaves, medium size
500 g topside, minced
250 g pork, minced
125 g chopped onion
¾ cup cooked rice
½ teaspoon cumin powder
1 egg
1 teaspoon thyme
1 tablespoon chopped parsley
1 clove garlic, chopped
1 tablespoon salt
¾ teaspoon pepper
2½ cups fresh tomato sauce (page 91)
¼ cup butter

Place cabbage leaves in 2 tablespoons water in a casserole dish. Cook covered for 8 minutes or until soft. Combine mince, pork, onion, rice, cumin, egg, thyme, parsley, garlic, salt, pepper, and ½ cup of tomato sauce. Place two tablespoons stuffing on each cabbage leaf and wrap leaves around mixture firmly. Place cabbage rolls in a casserole dish. Spread butter on top of rolls and remaining tomato sauce. Cook, covered, 20 minutes, or until meat is cooked and rolls are tender. Let stand, covered, 10 minutes.

POPCORN CRUNCH

TIME: 10 MINUTES (HIGH)	

1½ cups sugar
1 cup golden syrup
½ cup butter
8 cups popcorn, already popped
2 cups puffed wheat cereal
1 cup flaked almonds, toasted
¾ teaspoon cinnamon
1 teaspoon vanilla

Place sugar and golden syrup in a heatproof dish, stir and cook until sugar is dissolved, approximately 4 minutes on high. Add butter and cook for 6 minutes. Meanwhile, place popcorn, cereal and almonds into a separate bowl. Add cinnamon and vanilla to golden syrup mixture. Combine syrup with popcorn, cereal, and almonds, spread over base of lightly greased 25 cm x 30 cm baking tray. Allow to cool, break into pieces. Store in an airtight container. Note: Can be piled into ice cream cones for children's parties.

CREAM OF MUSHROOM SOUP

TIME: 17 MINUTES (HIGH)	SERVES 4

125 g mushrooms
4 tablespoons butter
4 tablespoons plain flour
1½ cups milk
1½ cups chicken stock
1 cup cream
salt and pepper
chopped chives

Slice and dice mushrooms. Place butter into a 2-litre casserole dish and cook 1 minute to melt. Add mushrooms, and cook covered 3 minutes. Stir in flour, cook a further 2 minutes. Blend in milk and stock. Cook 9 minutes on high. Add cream and cook 2 minutes to reheat. Season with salt and pepper. Add a few chopped chives before serving.

POPPED CORN

TIME: 16 MINUTES (HIGH)	

1 level tablespoon copha
½ cup popping corn
90 g butter, melted
½ level teaspoon salt

Heat copha in a round pyrex casserole in oven until a few corn grains spin slowly (approximately 10 minutes). Add corn and cook covered for 6 minutes. When popping ceases, remove from oven and toss in butter and salt. Yields 6 cups.

ANCHOVY BREAD

TIME: 1½ MINUTES (HIGH)

1 loaf French bread
1 small can anchovy fillets
finely chopped parsley
90 g butter

Mash anchovies with butter and parsley. Cut bread into slices ¾ through the loaf. Spread slices with butter. As the loaf will be too long for the microwave oven, cut loaf into four sections. Cook for 1½ minutes. Serve hot.

BACON AND OYSTER ROLLS

TIME: 6 MINUTES (HIGH)

6 narrow strips of bacon
12 fresh oysters, pierced with toothpick
toothpicks

Remove rind from bacon. Cut rasher in half. Cook between white kitchen paper for 3 minutes until partly cooked. Drain oysters. Wrap each bacon rasher around an oyster and fasten with a toothpick. Cook between layers of kitchen paper 2-3 minutes or until bacon becomes crisp. Note: Smoked oysters may also be used.

PARTY PIZZAS

TIME: 6 MINUTES (HIGH)

Lebanese bread

SAUCE
250 g can tomato paste
1 teaspoon sugar
½ teaspoon oregano
½ teaspoon freshly ground
   black pepper
½ teaspoon basil
} Combine

Have sauce prepared and the toppings arranged on a serving platter for guests to make their own selection.

Method:
Spread sauce over each bread round, add toppings and cook 6 minutes. Cut into wedges.

TOPPING SUGGESTIONS
fresh mushrooms, sliced
onion rings
mozzarella cheese slices
capsicum rings
rolled or flat anchovies
ham, strips
sliced continental salami
black or green stuffed olives
parmesan, cayenne, paprika
grated tasty cheese
parsley

Party Pizzas

SPINACH PIE

TIME: 15 MINUTES (HIGH) | SERVES 6

500 g precooked spinach leaves (see vegetable section)
1 onion, finely chopped
3 eggs
125 g fetta cheese
1 cup cottage cheese
2 tablespoons parmesan cheese
¼ cup parsley, chopped
salt and pepper
¼ teaspoon nutmeg
1 package filo pastry
½ cup butter, melted

Combine spinach, onion, eggs, cheese, parsley and seasonings into a bowl. Brush an oblong casserole dish with melted butter. Place 1 sheet of pastry into the dish so that it comes up to the top edges. Brush with melted butter and repeat until the base has 6-8 layers. Cook on high 2 minutes. Add filling to pastry, spreading evenly. Top with 6 more layers of buttered pastry. Trim edges. Cut into squares through the first four layers of pastry. Cook uncovered in oven for 13 minutes. Cut into squares and serve warm.

Optional: Brown top of pie under heated grill for 2-3 minutes.

TUNA OR SALMON MORNAY

TIME: 10 MINUTES (HIGH) | SERVES 4

2 cups tuna or salmon
2 cups white sauce (see sauce section)
125 g tasty cheese, grated
4 lemon wedges

Layer half tuna, half sauce, and half cheese in a 20 cm × 20 cm baking dish. Repeat second layer. Cook 10 minutes. Garnish with parsley, paprika and lemon wedges.

CHINESE CHICKEN SAVOURIES

TIME: 9 MINUTES (HIGH) | SERVES 4

2 double chicken breasts
1 tablespoon oil
30 g butter
1 tablespoon ginger, finely chopped
2-3 cloves garlic, crushed
2 tablespoons soy sauce

Remove chicken from bone. Cut into 2 cm pieces. Melt butter and oil in a pyrex pie dish. Add the ginger and garlic. Cook 1 minute. Add chicken pieces and soy sauce. Cover with plastic food wrap. Cook for 8 minutes. Stir halfway through cooking period. Do not overcook as chicken will toughen.

CHILLI CON CARNE

TIME: 13 MINUTES (HIGH) | SERVES 6

½ tablespoon butter
500 g topside, minced
1 small onion, diced
½ teaspoon garlic salt
1 tablespoon chilli powder
½ teaspoon dry mustard
salt and pepper
½ can tomatoes
250 g can kidney beans
250 g can baked beans
250 g can sliced mushrooms
2 stalks celery, diced
2 tablespoons tomato paste
1 teaspoon paprika
½ teaspoon oregano

Place butter, beef, diced onions and garlic salt into a 2-litre casserole dish. Cook 3 minutes until brown. Add chilli powder, mustard, pepper, salt and remaining ingredients. Cook for 10 minutes stirring after the first 5 minutes. Serve with rice or buttered toast.

Meat

Beef Olives

Meat should be roasted on a roasting rack in a shallow glass baking dish. Always cover the meat with white kitchen paper to prevent splattering.

Never use salt before roasting as this dehydrates the meat.

Large roasts will brown in a microwave oven but smaller portions will not brown. To give the surface a browned appearance apply a sauce or a baste: try soy sauce, teriyaki, or Worcestershire sauce. These add colour and flavour.

For steaks and chops, use your browning skillet as suggested in the recipes.

The internal temperature of the meat can be checked by inserting a meat thermometer into the thickest part, away from bone and fat. However, you must use a meat thermometer specially designed for use in a microwave oven.

When the meat has finished cooking, take it out of the oven and cover it with foil. Then allow it to stand for 15–20 minutes to equalise the heat.

BEEF OLIVES

TIME: 30 MINUTES (HIGH)	SERVES 3-4

500 g very thinly sliced rump steak
1 rasher bacon, diced
1 small onion, chopped
¼ cup breadcrumbs
1 tablespoon parsley, chopped
1 teaspoon lemon rind, grated
1 small carrot, grated
black pepper
¼ teaspoon salt
1 egg
seasoned flour
30 g butter
150 ml brown stock
150 ml red wine

Cut steak into 10 cm squares. Pound with meat mallet. Place bacon and onion into bowl, cook 3 minutes. Add breadcrumbs, parsley, lemon rind, carrot, pepper, salt, and egg. Blend together. Spread filling over meat slices. Roll up and tie with string. Coat meat with seasoned flour. Preheat browning skillet 6 minutes. Add butter to melt. Add beef rolls, cook 3 minutes on each side. Add stock, wine and cook covered 12 minutes medium. Remove string from rolls, transfer to serving plate. Add 3 teaspoons arrowroot blended with 1 tablespoon cold water to skillet juices. Cook on high 2-3 minutes to form sauce. Mask rolls with sauce. Sprinkle with cut parsley.

SEASONED SHOULDER OF LAMB

TIME: 39 MINUTES (HIGH)	SERVES 4-6

1 boned shoulder of lamb—2 kg
Cooking time 8-9 minutes per 500 g

SEASONING
1 cup fresh breadcrumbs
1 tablespoon butter
¼ teaspoon nutmeg
¼ teaspoon salt
¼ teaspoon pepper
1 tablespoon mint, chopped
pinch mixed herbs
2 tablespoons milk
2 shallots, finely cut
½ cup fresh mushrooms, sliced

} Combine

Place seasoning on boned lamb. Roll up. Tie firmly with string or fasten with bamboo satay sticks. Place onto roasting rack, fat side down. Cook 18 minutes, turn for remainder of cooking time. Wrap in foil for 15 minutes before carving. Serve with peach sauce.

PEACH SAUCE
1 cup cranberry sauce
½ cup diced peaches
2 tablespoons sweet vermouth or sherry

Combine and cook 3 minutes to heat.

ROAST PORK

TIME: 45 MINUTES (HIGH)	SERVES 6

2.5 kg leg or loin of pork in one piece
3 tablespoons oil
1 teaspoon salt
1 teaspoon five spice powder
juice of half a lemon

Cooking time, 8-9 minutes per 500 g. Score rind of pork. Brush with oil. Rub salt and five spice powder into the skin and allow to stand for 15 minutes. Pour lemon juice over. Place on roasting rack in casserole dish and cook 40-45 minutes. (It is not necessary to turn pork over during cooking.) Wrap in foil and allow to stand 20 minutes before carving. During last 4 minutes of cooking, place slices of apple and pineapple around pork. Glaze slices with apricot jam.

GUARD OF HONOUR

TIME: 23 MINUTES (HIGH)	SERVES 4-6

2 racks of lamb, each with 8 cutlets
cooking time: 8 minutes per 500 g

STUFFING
60 g butter
1 small onion, chopped finely
2 cups fresh breadcrumbs
1 tablespoon parsley, chopped
pinch dry mixed herbs
1 egg, beaten
1 teaspoon grated lemon or orange rind
garlic slivers

Place butter into bowl for 15-20 seconds to melt. Add onion and cook 2-3 minutes. Combine with remaining ingredients.

Interlace cutlet bones to form an arch. Stud with garlic slivers and season lightly. Place seasoning in centre of cutlet racks, and fasten with bamboo satay sticks to retain shape. Cook 20 minutes. Cover with foil and allow to stand 10-15 minutes. Top cutlet bones with frills. Serve with minted potato balls, honeyed carrots and a green vegetable (see vegetable section).

POTATO PIE

TIME: 12 MINUTES (HIGH)	SERVES 4-6

2 tablespoons butter
1 small onion, chopped finely
500 g cold roast lamb, minced
2 tablespoons parsley, chopped
250 g peas, cooked
250 g cooked carrots, sliced
250 g fresh mushrooms, sliced
1 teaspoon curry powder
1 (165 g) can mushroom soup
salt and pepper
2 cups hot mashed potato
nutmeg and paprika

Melt butter in casserole dish for 15 seconds. Add onion and cook 3 minutes. Fold in lamb, parsley, peas, carrots, mushrooms, curry powder, soup, salt and pepper. Pipe potatoes over top of mixture. Sprinkle with nutmeg and paprika. Cook 9 minutes.

GARLIC BRAINS

TIME: 16 MINUTES (HIGH)	SERVES 2-4

500 g calves' or lambs' brains
1 tablespoon white wine
45 g butter
4 cloves garlic
juice of ½ lemon
chopped parsley
seasoning salt

Trim and rinse brains. Place in flat dish and add 1 tablespoon of dry white wine. Cover with plastic food wrap and cook 4 minutes on high. Turn over after 2 minutes. Cool and cut into thick slices. Heat browning skillet for 6 minutes. Add butter and chopped garlic. Cook 2 minutes. Add sliced brains and cook 2 minutes on each side. Add lemon juice, chopped parsley, seasoning salt.

VIENNA SCHNITZEL

TIME: 15 MINUTES (HIGH)	SERVES 2-3

500 g fillets of veal
¼ cup lemon juice
seasoned flour
1 egg, beaten
2 tablespoons milk   } Combine
1 teaspoon soy sauce
1 cup breadcrumbs
1 cup oil
lemon wedges

Pound veal fillets with meat mallet until thin. Marinate in lemon juice for 20 minutes. Dust with seasoned flour, dip into egg mixture, and coat with breadcrumbs. Preheat browning skillet for 8 minutes. Add oil and heat for 3 minutes. Add schnitzels, cook 2 minutes on each side. Serve with lemon wedges.

LAMB CASSEROLE

TIME: 47 MINUTES (MEDIUM)　　　　SERVES 4

750 g lean lamb
3 tablespoons flour
salt and pepper　} Combine
oregano
pinch of thyme
60 g butter
1 large onion, chopped finely
2 carrots, sliced
250 g potato balls
½ red capsicum, diced
bouquet garni
1½ cups beef stock

Cut lamb into even sized pieces, roll in seasoned flour. Heat browning skillet for 8 minutes. Add butter to melt. Add lamb pieces, cook 2 minutes on each side. Add all vegetables and bouquet garni, cook covered 5 minutes on high, stirring once during cooking. Add stock, cook covered on medium for 35 minutes. Let stand 10-15 minutes before serving.

ROAST LEG OF LAMB

TIME: 53 MINUTES (HIGH)　　　　SERVES 8

Weigh leg of lamb and allow 8 minutes per 500 g cooking time.

1 (2.5 kg) leg of lamb
3 cloves garlic, peeled
lemon-flavoured black pepper
1 teaspoon powdered ginger
variety of vegetables
1 can drained pears
1 jar mint jelly

Trim excess fat from lamb. Cut garlic in slivers and stud lamb. Sprinkle with lemon-flavoured black pepper and rub lightly with ginger. Place lamb, fat side down, on a roasting rack in an oblong casserole dish or just place into casserole dish. Cover with a sheet of white kitchen paper and cook 25 minutes. Turn leg over and baste with pan drippings. Cook a further 15 minutes. Wrap in foil, allow to stand for 15 minutes before carving. During this time vegetables can be cooked in the baking dish. Suggested vegetables: whole onions, sweet potato, pumpkin, potatoes. Place vegetables into pan and baste with drippings. Cook 5 minutes. Turn over to cook a further 5 minutes or until tender. Fill pears with mint jelly and heat 3 minutes.

BEEF STROGANOFF

TIME: 25 MINUTES (HIGH & MEDIUM)　　SERVES 4-6

2 tablespoons oil
500 g rump steak
½ teaspoon salt
½ teaspoon pepper　} Combine
2 tablespoons flour
2 onions, sliced
1 clove garlic, cut finely
250 g fresh mushrooms, sliced
150 ml red wine
150 ml beef stock
1 tablespoon tomato paste
1 carton sour cream

Preheat browning skillet for 8 minutes. Add oil and heat for 2 minutes. Cut meat into very thin slices, across grain. Roll in seasoned flour. Add to pan and cook 3-4 minutes, stirring frequently to brown meat. Add onions, garlic and cook 3 minutes. Add mushrooms, wine, stock, tomato paste and cook 6 minutes on medium. Blend in sour cream, cook to reheat 2 minutes. Serve with rice or buttered noodles.

ROAST PORK RIBS

TIME: 20 MINUTES (HIGH)   SERVES 4

750 g pork spareribs
1 medium onion, chopped ⎤
2 tablespoons dark soy sauce
3 tablespoons honey
2 tablespoons lemon juice
1 clove garlic, crushed
¼ teaspoon salt   ⎬ Marinade
pinch pepper
½ teaspoon curry powder
¼ teaspoon chilli powder
½ teaspoon ground ginger
¼ cup oil   ⎦

Remove rind and excess fat from ribs. Prick with skewer and place into marinade for 2 hours. Place ribs onto a roasting rack and cook 20 minutes, turning after 10 minutes. Spare ribs may also be cooked in an oven bag. Note: Chicken wings can be cooked in this method.

Roast Pork Ribs

LAMB CURRY

TIME: 36 MINUTES (HIGH)	SERVES 4-6

750 g boneless leg of lamb
30 g butter
250 g onions, chopped
1 clove garlic, chopped
2 tablespoons curry powder
1 tablespoon flour
1 tablespoon chutney
2 teaspoons coconut
1 tablespoon sultanas
60 g chopped apple
2 tablespoons tomato paste
1 cup beef stock
salt

Trim lamb and cut into even sized pieces. Preheat browning skillet 6 minutes. Add butter and heat for 2 minutes. Cook lamb pieces 3 minutes on each side with onion and garlic. Drain off any fat, add curry powder and flour. Mix well and cook 2 minutes. Add chutney, coconut, sultanas, apples, tomato paste and stock. Cook covered 20 minutes on high, stirring occasionally. Serve with plain boiled rice and cucumber sambal.

CORNED SILVERSIDE

TIME: 1-2 HOURS (See Instructions)	SERVES 6-8

4 cups boiling water
1.5 kg corned silverside
3 cloves
1 small onion, chopped
1 cinnamon stick
¼ teaspoon nutmeg
1 tablespoon brown sugar
1 bay leaf
1 tablespoon vinegar

DEFROST COOKING CYCLE METHOD — TIME: 2 HOURS
Place water, meat and remaining ingredients into a covered casserole dish and cook on *Defrost Cycle* 1¾-2 hours, or until tender when pierced with a fork. Allow to stand 10 minutes before carving.

OVEN BAG METHOD — TIME: 1 HOUR (HIGH & MEDIUM)
Soak beef in 2 changes of cold water for 2 hours. Place meat into an oven bag with remaining ingredients and 1½ cups of cold water. Tie bag. Place into large pyrex bowl. Pierce bag once or twice. Cook 30 minutes on high, turn meat over and cook 30 minutes on medium. Allow to stand 10 minutes before carving.

VEAL MARSALA

TIME: 14 MINUTES (HIGH)	SERVES 4

500 g veal steak
seasoned flour
3 tablespoons butter
½ cup Marsala

Pound veal with mallet to flatten. Dust with seasoned flour. Heat browning skillet 6 minutes. Add butter to melt. Add veal and cook 2 minutes on each side. Add Marsala and cook 3-4 minutes to form a sauce with pan drippings.

VEAL CORDON BLEU

TIME: 19 MINUTES (HIGH)	SERVES 2

4 × 125 g slices veal
2 slices Gruyere cheese
2 slices lean ham
seasoned flour
1 beaten egg ⎫
1 tablespoon milk ⎬ Combine
1 teaspoon soy sauce ⎭
1 cup seasoned breadcrumbs

Pound veal slices with mallet until thin. Place 1 slice each of cheese and ham onto 2 veal slices. Top with remaining veal. Seal outer edges of veal by tapping with meat mallet. Dust with seasoned flour, dip into egg mixture and coat with breadcrumbs. Preheat browning skillet 8 minutes. Add oil and heat for 3 minutes. Cook veal for 4 minutes on each side.

PEPPER STEAK

TIME: 17 MINUTES (HIGH)	SERVES 4

4 thin slices fillet steak
2 tablespoons ground black pepper
2 tablespoons oil
2 cloves garlic, chopped finely
2 tablespoons brandy
¼ cup white wine

Cover steaks with ground pepper and pound with mallet. Heat browning skillet for 6 minutes. Add oil and garlic. Heat for 3 minutes. Press steak into pan, cook 3 minutes on each side. Add brandy and wine, cook 2 minutes.

BRAISED PORK CHOPS

TIME: 23 MINUTES (HIGH)	SERVES 4

4 shoulder pork chops
seasoned flour
2 tablespoons oil
1 onion, sliced
3 large mushrooms, sliced
2 tomatoes, peeled and sliced
½ cup chicken stock
½ cup port wine
2 cloves
salt and pepper

Coat chops with seasoned flour. Heat browning skillet for 6 minutes. Add oil and heat for 3 minutes. Press chops into skillet and cook 3 minutes on each side to brown. Add onion, mushrooms, tomato, stock, port, cloves, salt and pepper. Cover and cook for 8 minutes. Allow to stand 5 minutes before serving. Sauce may be thickened lightly with cornflour.

MEAT LOAF

TIME: 25 MINUTES (HIGH)	SERVES 4-6

2 bread slices, 1 cm thick
500 g minced topside
60 g onion, chopped finely
60 g green capsicum, chopped finely
60 g celery, chopped finely
½ cup grated tasty cheese
1 tablespoon parsley, chopped
125 ml tomato juice
2 eggs
¾ teaspoon salt
dash of pepper and nutmeg
2 tablespoons Worcestershire sauce
60 g tomato sauce

Soak bread slices in water until soft. Squeeze out water thoroughly. Mix mince, bread, onion, green capsicum, celery, cheese, parsley and tomato juice in a bowl. Stir well. Add eggs, salt, pepper and nutmeg. Stir well again. Shape meat into a loaf and place in dish. Cook 20 minutes. Blend Worcestershire sauce and tomato sauce. Drizzle liquid over top of loaf. Cook 5 minutes.
Note: Fruit chutney and extra grated cheese can be spread on top of meat loaf during last 5 minutes of cooking.

Poultry

Braised Lemon Chicken

Poultry cooked in a microwave oven has a delicate flavour and is very tender and juicy.

Whole or large pieces of poultry will brown easily in a microwave oven, but smaller portions can be browned by searing either in a fry pan, under the grill, or in the microwave browning skillet.

Never season poultry with salt before roasting as this tends to dehydrate the flesh and make it tough. Other herbs and spices may, however, be used.

Place poultry portions in a shallow dish wide enough to lay them flat in a single layer for even heat penetration. Always arrange the portions having the most flesh near the edge of the dish and place bones, such as drumstick ends, wings and backs, in the centre of the dish.

When cooking, always cover chicken pieces with white kitchen paper to prevent splattering.

BRAISED LEMON CHICKEN

TIME: 52 MINUTES (HIGH)	SERVES 4-6

2 tablespoons dark soy sauce
1 tablespoon dry sherry
1 cup lemon juice
2 teaspoons sugar
1 kg chicken breasts, cut into serving
   pieces
3 tablespoons oil
2 thin slices of green ginger
1 clove garlic, peeled and crushed
¾ cup water
1 tablespoon cornflour
salt
2-3 tablespoons water

Mix soy sauce, sherry, lemon juice, sugar in a bowl. Add chicken pieces and marinate for 20 minutes. Preheat browning skillet for 6 minutes. Add oil and heat for 2 minutes. Add ginger, garlic, chicken pieces and cook 3 minutes on each side. Place chicken, garlic and ginger into a casserole dish. Add remaining marinade and water. Cook covered 15-18 minutes, stirring twice during cooking. Add blended cornflour, cook 2 minutes. Season. Serve with plain boiled rice.

SPANISH CHICKEN

TIME: 36 MINUTES (HIGH)	SERVES 4-6

1 kg chicken breasts, cut into pieces
seasoned flour, salt and pepper
4 tablespoons oil
2 onions, chopped
1 clove garlic, crushed
2 tablespoons parsley, chopped
2 tablespoons shallots, chopped
4 tomatoes, sliced
1 green capsicum, chopped
125 g button mushrooms
1¼ cups red wine
1 teaspoon red chilli, finely chopped
salt
pepper
1 cup frozen lima beans, cooked

Toss chicken pieces in seasoned flour. Preheat browning skillet for 6 minutes. Add 2 tablespoons oil and heat a further 2 minutes. Place chicken pieces in skillet and cook 3 minutes on each side. Place chicken pieces into a 2 litre casserole dish. Reheat browning skillet for 2 minutes, add onions, garlic, remaining oil and cook for 2 minutes. Remove and add to chicken. Add parsley, shallots, tomatoes, capsicum, mushrooms, wine, chilli, salt and pepper. Cover casserole and cook 15 minutes. Add cooked beans and cook a further 3 minutes. Serve with boiled rice.

MEXICAN CHICKEN

TIME: 35 MINUTES (HIGH)	SERVES 4-6

1 large chicken, jointed, or chicken
   pieces
seasoned flour
4 tablespoons oil
3 large onions, sliced
2 cloves garlic, crushed
1 red capsicum, diced
1 tablespoon sesame seeds
½ teaspoon oregano
¾ cup dry red wine
1 cup blanched almonds
1 cup stuffed olives, sliced
½-1 teaspoon chilli powder
1 cup chicken stock
1 cup whole kernel corn

Dust chicken pieces lightly with seasoned flour. Preheat browning skillet for 6 minutes. Add oil, heat for 2 minutes. Add chicken pieces and cook for 3 minutes on each side. Remove chicken and place into a 2 litre casserole dish. Place onions, garlic, capsicum, into browning skillet and cook 3 minutes, stirring after 2 minutes. Add sesame seeds, oregano, wine and pour over chicken pieces. Add almonds, olives, chilli powder, stock, and cook covered 15 minutes. Fold in corn kernels and cook 3 minutes longer.

APRICOT CHICKEN CASSEROLE

TIME: 37 MINUTES (HIGH)   SERVES 4-6

3 tablespoons oil
1 kg chicken breasts, cut into serving
    pieces
2 tablespoons butter
1 large onion, diced
1 green capsicum, diced
2 tablespoons plain flour
1½ cups apricot nectar
salt and pepper
pinch oregano
2 teaspoons parsley, chopped
3 large tomatoes, peeled and sliced

Preheat browning skillet for 6 minutes. Add oil and heat for 2 minutes. Add chicken pieces and cook for 3 minutes on each side. Melt butter in a 2 litre casserole for 15 seconds. Add onion, capsicum and cook for 3 minutes. Stir in flour and cook for 2 minutes. Stir in apricot nectar to form a sauce. Add browned chicken pieces and remaining seasonings. Cover with tomato slices. Cook covered 18 minutes. Serve with buttered, boiled macaroni, which has been sprinkled with toasted sesame seeds.

CHICKEN IN RED WINE

TIME: 39 MINUTES (HIGH)   SERVES 4-6

1 chicken, cut in serving pieces
60 g seasoned flour
3 tablespoons oil
120 g bacon, diced
1 clove garlic, chopped
6 small onions
2 cups red wine
120 g button mushrooms
salt and pepper

Coat chicken pieces lightly with seasoned flour. Preheat browning skillet for 6 minutes. Add oil and heat for 2 minutes. Place in chicken pieces pressing down on all sides to seal and colour. Cook 3 minutes on each side. Remove chicken from pan and place into a 2 litre casserole dish. Reheat browning skillet for 4 minutes, add bacon, garlic and onions, cover with kitchen paper and cook for 3 minutes. Add this mixture to chicken. Gradually blend in wine with remaining flour to form a smooth paste. Add mushrooms and cook covered 15-18 minutes, stirring twice during cooking.

GOURMET CHICKEN

TIME: 38 MINUTES (HIGH)   SERVES 4

2 whole chicken breasts
seasoned flour
3 tablespoons oil
¼ cup blanched slivered almonds
1 small onion, diced
1 clove garlic, minced
1 cup celery, diced
2 tablespoons parsley, minced
¾ cup dry sherry
1 cup button mushrooms
parsley sprigs for garnish
1 tablespoon cornflour (optional)

Cut chicken breasts into serving pieces and dust lightly with seasoned flour. Preheat browning skillet for 6 minutes. Add oil and heat for 2 minutes. Add almonds, brown slightly, set aside for garnish. Reheat skillet for 2 minutes, add chicken pieces and cook 3 minutes on each side. Remove chicken and place into a 2-litre casserole dish. Place onion, garlic, celery, parsley into browning skillet and cook 2 minutes. Add sherry, mushrooms and stir well. Pour mixture over chicken pieces and cook covered 15-18 minutes. Thicken lightly with cornflour if necessary and cook 2 minutes longer. Serve garnished with almonds and parsley sprigs.

CRUMBED CHICKEN DRUMSTICKS

MICROWAVE TIME: 8 MINUTES (HIGH) SERVES 4

2 cups cooking oil
1 clove garlic, peeled and crushed
8 drumsticks
4 tablespoons plain flour ⎫
salt and pepper   ⎪
pinch oregano   ⎬ Combine
½ level teaspoon five   ⎪
    spice powder   ⎭
1 egg   ⎫ lightly beaten
¼ cup milk   ⎭
1½ cups dry breadcrumbs ⎫ Combine
¼ cup sesame seeds   ⎭

Heat oil in pan on top of range. Add garlic, brown and remove. Roll drumsticks in seasoned flour. Coat with egg mixture, then with breadcrumb mixture. Fry drumsticks until a rich golden colour. Remove and drain. Arrange on a glass platter with the thickest part of the drumstick to the outside edge. Cover with white kitchen paper. Cook for 8 minutes, turn over after 5 minutes of cooking. Serve with rice.

Note: This method combines the crispness of pan frying with the moist cooking of the microwave oven.

Crumbed Chicken Drumsticks

RED ROAST CHICKEN

| TIME: 25 MINUTES (HIGH) | SERVES 4-6 |

1 whole chicken
1 slice ginger
1 clove garlic, crushed
MARINADE
¾ cup Chinese
   barbecue sauce
pinch red food
   colouring powder } Combine in a bowl
½ cup dry sherry

Place ginger and crushed garlic into cavity of chicken. Coat chicken with marinade and allow to stand for 2 hours. Place chicken into an oven bag. Tie loosely with string. Prick bag once or twice. Place into a casserole dish and cook 15 minutes. Turn over and cook a further 10 minutes. Allow to stand 10 minutes before carving. Serve hot or cold with salads.

SWEET AND SOUR CHICKEN

| TIME: 34 MINUTES (HIGH) | SERVES 4-6 |

750 g fresh chicken breasts
3 tablespoons oil
1 clove garlic, chopped finely
1 thin slice ginger, chopped finely

SAUCE
½ cup sugar
½ cup vinegar
¾ cup pineapple juice or water
1-2 tablespoons dark soy sauce
2 tablespoons oil
1 clove garlic, chopped finely
½ red capsicum, diced
½ green capsicum, diced
¼ cup Chinese pickles, diced
¼ cup mushrooms, sliced
¼ cup bamboo shoots, sliced
3 shallots, cut into 2 cm lengths
2 tablespoons cornflour blended with
   ½ cup water

Remove flesh from bone and cut into 2 cm dice. Preheat browning skillet for 8 minutes. Add oil and heat for 3 minutes. Add garlic, ginger and cook 1 minute. Add chicken pieces and stir to coat with oil. Cook 5 minutes, stir and cook a further 5 minutes.

Combine sugar, vinegar, pineapple juice, and soy sauce. Heat oil in casserole dish for 2 minutes. Add garlic, vegetables and cook for 3 minutes uncovered. Add vinegar mixture. Cook for 3 minutes. Blend cornflour and water to a paste. Add to other ingredients and cook for 2 minutes. Add chicken pieces. Reheat for 2 minutes. Serve with plain or fried rice.

CHILLI CHICKEN

| TIME: 20 MINUTES (HIGH) | SERVES 4 |

2 whole chicken breasts, cut into
   serving pieces
4 red chillies, seeds removed and
   chopped finely
2 slices green ginger, chopped finely
2 cloves garlic, chopped finely
1 medium onion, chopped finely
2 teaspoons lemon or lime juice
1 teaspoon turmeric
1 teaspoon sugar
salt

Salt chicken pieces lightly. Combine all other ingredients in a bowl. Add chicken pieces and allow to stand 15-20 minutes. Place chicken and marinade in an oven bag. Tie bag loosely with string or elastic band. Cook 10 minutes, then turn bag over and continue cooking a further 10 minutes.
Note: The chicken in the oven bag must be in one layer, not bunched up.

ROAST CHICKEN

TIME: 33 MINUTES (HIGH)	SERVES 4-6

1 large chicken, size 16, washed and
dried

STUFFING
1 small onion, chopped finely
1 cup white breadcrumbs
pinch of mixed herbs
1 tablespoon butter
¼ teaspoon salt
pinch pepper
1 tablespoon parsley, chopped

BASTING SAUCE
1-2 tablespoons melted butter
1 teaspoon soy sauce

Saute onion in butter, 3 minutes on high. Add remaining ingredients. Place stuffing into cavity. Truss chicken to a neat shape. Baste with 2 tablespoons melted butter mixed with 1 teaspoon soy sauce. Place into an oven bag. Tie loosely with string and prick bag once or twice. Cook 15 minutes, breast side down. Turn over and cook a further 15 minutes. Let stand in bag for 10 minutes before carving. Note: Baked rabbit can also be cooked in this way.

CHICKEN SATAY

TIME: 16 MINUTES (HIGH)	SERVES 4-6

500 g chicken breasts
1 cup pineapple pieces
1 cup button mushrooms
1 cup red capsicum diced same size as
    pineapple
MARINADE
3 tablespoons soy sauce
1 tablespoon dry sherry
1 tablespoon brown
    sugar
½ teaspoon powdered
    ginger
2 teaspoons grated onion
} Combine in a bowl, add chicken pieces and marinate for 1 hour.
SAUCE
1 cup pineapple juice
1 tablespoon cornflour
} Combine

Debone chicken. Cut into 2 cm cubes. Marinate 1 hour. Arrange chicken pieces, pineapple and vegetables on bamboo skewers. Preheat browning skillet for 8 minutes. Add 2 tablespoons oil and heat for 2 minutes. Arrange skewers in oil and cook 3 minutes, turn and cook a further 3 minutes. Place on serving platter. Heat pineapple juice and cornflour to form a sauce. Spoon over satays and serve.

ROAST ORANGE DUCK

TIME: 33 MINUTES (HIGH)	SERVES 4

1 duck, 2 kg
1 clove garlic
2 tablespoons butter, melted and mixed
    with 2 teaspoons soy sauce
1 onion, peeled and cut into quarters
1 orange, unpeeled, cut into quarters
¼ cup dry sherry
½ cup orange juice
½ teaspoon ground ginger
1 teaspoon salt
parsley
1 tablespoon cornflour
2 tablespoons water

Wipe duck inside and out with a damp cloth. Cut garlic in half and rub skin with it. Brush with butter and soy mixture. Place onion and orange into cavity and fasten with a bamboo satay stick. Place duck into a shallow glass baking dish. Cover loosely with plastic food wrap and cook 15 minutes. Pour sherry, orange juice, ginger and salt over duck. Re-cover and cook a further 15 minutes. Allow to stand 10 minutes. Remove orange and onion. Blend 1 tablespoon cornflour with a little water and add to pan drippings. Cook a further 3 minutes. Carve duck and garnish with orange segments and parsley. Mask with thickened orange sauce.
Note: The duck can also be cooked in an oven bag.

ROAST TURKEY

TIME: 80 MINUTES (HIGH) SERVES 8-10

1 turkey, approximately 5 kg

Cooking times
16 minutes per kilo (high)
24 minutes per kilo (medium)

Clean and prepare turkey for cooking. Place turkey, breast side down in a glass baking dish. Put apple dressing inside cavity of turkey. Cover bottom half of wings and legs with small pieces of aluminium foil. Secure legs and wings close to body with string. Cover turkey lightly with plastic food wrap—this keeps the inside tender and juicy. Cook turkey for 40 minutes then remove foil, turn turkey over, cover and cook a further 40 minutes. When cooking time is up, rest turkey 15-20 minutes before carving.
Note: If turkey cavity is filled with apple dressing, add 2 minutes per kilo to cooking time.

APPLE DRESSING

TIME: 3 MINUTES (HIGH)

1 cup butter
1½ cups celery, finely chopped
¾ cup onion, finely chopped
1 teaspoon salt
1 teaspoon sage
½ - ¾ cup water
5 cups dry breadcrumbs, more if needed
3 cups peeled and chopped apple

Melt butter in a large casserole, saute celery and onion 2-3 minutes, stirring after every minute. Mix salt, sage, and water together. Pour over breadcrumbs and toss lightly. Add breadcrumbs to vegetables, and stir in apples. Stuff turkey just before roasting.

ALTERNATIVE STUFFING FOR TURKEY

STUFFING FOR CAVITY
125 g butter
60 g onion, finely chopped
125 g fresh white breadcrumbs
fresh or dry mixed herbs
1 tablespoon parsley, chopped
turkey liver, chopped
salt and pepper

Place butter and onion into casserole dish or bowl. Cook 4 minutes, add remaining ingredients, mix well and place into cavity. Truss turkey firmly. A small amount of foil may be placed on the wings and drumsticks for half of the cooking time to prevent drying out. Cover the whole turkey with plastic wrap to retain natural juices.

STUFFING FOR NECK CAVITY
500 g sausage mince
125 g water chestnuts, diced
salt and pepper

Combine ingredients and place into neck cavity. Fasten with bamboo satay stick.

Roast Turkey

Seafood

Oysters Kilpatrick

Cooking fish or shellfish in a microwave oven is very rewarding. As it takes only minutes to be cooked to perfection, fish must be watched carefully during the cooking period. Overcooking toughens the fish and destroys its delicate flavour. Fish should only be cooked until it can be easily flaked with a fork.

To ensure even cooking, arrange the fish with the thickest portions near to the edge of the dish. Turn each portion over about halfway through the cooking period.

OYSTERS KILPATRICK

TIME: 5 MINUTES (HIGH)	SERVES 1-2

12 oysters on the shell
4 rashers bacon, diced without rind
2-3 tablespoons Worcestershire sauce
salt and pepper

Wash oysters and shell to remove any grit. Dry with a clean cloth. Place diced bacon onto a sheet of white kitchen paper. Cover with a second piece of paper. Microwave cook 3 minutes. Pierce oysters with toothpick. Top with bacon. Sprinkle with sauce. Season to taste. Cook 1-2 minutes.

OYSTERS MORNAY

TIME: 6 MINUTES (HIGH)	SERVES 1-2

12 oysters on the shell. Pierce oysters with toothpick before cooking.

SAUCE
2 tablespoons butter
2 tablespoons plain flour
1⅓ cups milk
¼ cup parmesan cheese, grated
¼ cup Swiss cheese, grated

Put butter into small ovenproof dish and cook 15 seconds to melt. Stir in flour, then milk. Cook 3 minutes or until mixture boils. Stir sauce after 1 minute. Stir in cheese. Cover and cook until cheese melts. Spoon sauce over each oyster on the shell. Dust lightly with paprika, or a little extra grated cheese. Cook 1-2 minutes and serve with lemon wedges.

GARLIC PRAWNS

TIME: 4 MINUTES (HIGH)	SERVES 4

4-6 tablespoons peanut oil
4 cloves garlic, finely cut
2 shallots, finely cut
1 fresh hot red chilli, sliced without seeds, or ½ teaspoon chilli powder
500 g shelled green prawns

Combine oil, garlic, shallots and chilli in microwave oven dish. Add prawns and toss to coat with oil. Allow to stand 10 minutes. Cook in oven 2 minutes. Stir and cook until they turn pink, another 2 minutes.

FILLETS OF FLOUNDER WITH PERNOD SAUCE

TIME: 9 MINUTES (HIGH)	SERVES 4-6

20 g butter
6 fillets of flounder
fish seasoning
juice half a lemon
2 tablespoons Pernod
⅓ cup cream
sprinkling of dry basil
chopped chives

Melt butter in an oblong dish for 15 seconds. Sprinkle fillets lightly with seasoning and place into butter. Pour over lemon juice and Pernod. Cook covered in oven 6-7 minutes. Remove to plate, reheat liquids, add cream, basil and cook 1½ minutes. Spoon over fillets. Sprinkle with chopped chives and serve.

SALMON RING

TIME: 8½ MINUTES (HIGH)	SERVES 6

1 × 500 g can red salmon
½ cup chopped onion
¼ cup salad oil
⅓ cup dry breadcrumbs
2 eggs, beaten
1 teaspoon dry mustard
½ teaspoon salt

Drain salmon, reserving ⅓ cup liquid. Cook onion in oil for 2½ minutes. Combine onion, dry breadcrumbs, salmon liquid, eggs, mustard, salt and flaked salmon in a basin and mix well. Place into a microwave ring pan and cook for 6 minutes. Give pan a quarter of a turn after 3 minutes. Let stand for 5 minutes before serving.
Note: Tuna may be used instead of salmon.

SMOKED SALMON QUICHE

TIME: 31 MINUTES (HIGH & DEFROST)   SERVES 6

PASTRY
2 cups flour
1¼ cups butter
½ teaspoon salt
¼ cup cold water

Sift dry ingredients into a bowl. Rub in butter and mix to a firm dough with water. Knead lightly and roll out to fit a 21 cm pie plate. Chill for 15 minutes. Cook for 6 minutes on high.

CUSTARD
1 cup cream
4 egg yolks
2 shallots, finely chopped   } Blend together
salt, cayenne pepper, and nutmeg to taste
180 g smoked salmon, thinly sliced

Pour custard into cool pastry shell and carefully float salmon slices on the surface. With a teaspoon, carefully lift some of the custard over the top of the salmon. Bake on the *Defrost Cycle* for 25 minutes until centre is set. Stand 3 minutes before serving.

SALMON STUFFED MUSHROOMS

TIME: 5 MINUTES (HIGH)   SERVES 6

12 medium to large mushrooms
6 tablespoons flaked red salmon
6 tablespoons soft breadcrumbs
2 teaspoons shallots, finely chopped
2 teaspoons parsley, finely chopped
2 teaspoons lemon juice
2 tablespoons butter, melted
grated parmesan cheese

Remove stems from mushrooms. Chop stems finely. Combine salmon, breadcrumbs, stems, shallots, parsley, lemon juice and butter. Fill caps with mixture. Sprinkle with cheese. Arrange mushrooms in a circle on the outer edge of a glass platter. Cook 5 minutes on high.

WHOLE FISH WITH BLACK BEAN SAUCE

TIME: 11 MINUTES (HIGH)   SERVES 4-6

1 whole fish, approximately 750 g or fish fillets

SAUCE:
1 tablespoon oil
1 slice green ginger, cut finely
1 clove garlic, cut finely
1 tablespoon black beans
½ teaspoon dry sherry
½ teaspoon sugar
2 teaspoons soy sauce
1 cup fish stock or water
1 tablespoon cornflour
water
3 shallots, cut finely

Trim off fins and tail with a pair of scissors. Remove the eyes. Check that all scales have been removed. Wash well and dry with kitchen paper. A small amount of fish seasoning may be sprinkled into cavity. Place fish onto a plate and cover with plastic food wrap. Cook approximately 6-8 minutes or until flesh flakes easily.

Heat oil in a bowl for 2 minutes. Add ginger, garlic, beans, and stir. Cook for 1 minute. Add sherry, sugar, soy sauce and stock. Cook 1 minute. Blend cornflour and water, stir into mixture. Cook a further 2 minutes. Stir in shallots. Spoon over fish. Serve garnished with shredded red capsicum.

BAKED ORANGE FISH

TIME: 9½ MINUTES (HIGH)   SERVES 4

1 large orange
1 small clove garlic
1 tablespoon butter
1 small onion, finely cut
1 tablespoon parsley, finely chopped
salt and pepper
1 cup fresh bean sprouts, roots removed
¾ cup orange juice
1 whole fish (750 g to 1 kg)

Cooking time
5 minutes per 500 g

Peel orange and cut into segments. Cut garlic into small pieces and half the orange segments into dice. Place butter, onion, garlic, orange segments, parsley, salt and pepper into a microwave oven dish and cook covered for 2 minutes. Add bean sprouts. After trimming fins and tail, place fish on a baking dish, removing eyes and checking for any scales which may have been missed. If the fish is large it may be scored 2 or 3 times on each side to ensure even cooking. Season cavity with salt and pepper. Stuff cavity with onion and orange mixture. Cover fish with plastic wrap and cook 5 minutes. Pour juice over fish and arrange remaining segments over fish neatly. Continue cooking 2½ minutes until flesh flakes easily.

WHOLE FISH WITH CHINESE PICKLE SAUCE

TIME: 15 MINUTES (HIGH)   SERVES 4-6

1 whole fish, approximately 750 g
Cooking time 5 minutes per 500 g

CHINESE PICKLE SAUCE
2 teaspoons tomato sauce
½ teaspoon salt
2 teaspoons soy sauce
2 cups pineapple juice
½ cup Chinese mixed pickle, diced
1 slice pineapple, diced
2 tablespoons vinegar
3 tablespoons brown sugar
small piece capsicum, diced
1-2 tablespoons cornflour

Prepare and cook the fish in the same way as whole fish with black bean sauce.

Combine all ingredients in a bowl except cornflour. Cook 4-5 minutes until boiling. Stir after 3 minutes. Thicken with blended cornflour. Cook 2 minutes, serve over fish.

SCALLOPS IN OYSTER SAUCE

TIME: 7 MINUTES (HIGH)   SERVES 4

1½ tablespoons oil
1 slice green ginger, cut finely
1 clove garlic, cut finely
500 g scallops
1 tablespoon dry sherry
2 teaspoons soy sauce
½ cup fish stock
2 tablespoons oyster sauce
1 teaspoon sugar
3 teaspoons cornflour
2 shallots, cut into 2 cm lengths
½ teaspoon salt

Heat oil in ovenproof dish for 1 minute. Add ginger, garlic and scallops. Cook for 3 minutes. Add sherry, soy sauce and cook 1 minute. Blend the stock, oyster sauce, sugar and cornflour. Add to dish, stir to blend and cook 2 minutes until boiling. Fold in shallots, salt and serve with plain boiled rice.

COQUILLES ST. JACQUES

TIME: 9½ MINUTES (HIGH)   SERVES 4

1 tablespoon butter
1 small onion, finely chopped
250 g scallops
2 teaspoons lemon juice
½ teaspoon salt
marjoram
dash paprika
6 tablespoons white wine
3 tablespoons butter
2 tablespoons flour
½ cup cream
60 g mushrooms, sliced thinly
fresh white breadcrumbs
1 teaspoon parsley, chopped

Combine 1 tablespoon butter and onion in a medium casserole dish. Cook uncovered 1 minute. Stir in scallops, lemon juice, seasoning and wine. Cook, covered 3 minutes. Drain liquid and reserve. Melt 3 tablespoons butter for 30 seconds. Blend in flour then stir in reserved liquid and cream. Heat, uncovered, 2 minutes or until sauce thickens. Add scallop mixture, mushrooms and spoon into 4 individual ramekins, or scallop shells. Sprinkle with breadcrumbs and parsley and heat uncovered 3 minutes.

FRESH TROUT WITH ASPARAGUS SAUCE

TIME: 7 MINUTES (HIGH)   SERVES 2

2 whole trout, approximately 250 g
    each
2 small branches of fresh dill
fish seasoning
1 shallot, cut finely
1 tablespoon dry vermouth
4 tablespoons fish stock or white wine
1 lemon, peeled and sliced
butter

Wash and dry trout, remove eyes. Place fresh dill into cavities and season. Place into a glass dish, sprinkle with shallots, vermouth, fish stock and cover with slices of lemon. Dot lightly with butter. Cover with plastic food wrap and cook 6-7 minutes.

ASPARAGUS SAUCE

TIME: 2 MINUTES (HIGH)   SERVES 2

1 (340 g) can green asparagus spears
8 tablespoons chicken stock
salt and pepper
1 tablespoon fresh cream

Combine asparagus with stock, salt, pepper and cream. Puree in a blender until smooth. Correct seasonings. Pour into glass jug. Cook 2 minutes. Mask trout with sauce.

CURRIED PRAWNS

TIME: 13 MINUTES (HIGH)   SERVES 4-6

2 tablespoons butter
1 tablespoon fresh ginger, grated
¼ cup minced onion
¼ cup plain flour
1 tablespoon curry powder
1 cup milk
1 cup coconut milk
2 teaspoons lemon juice
500 g green prawns

Place butter, ginger and onion in a 2½ quart casserole and cook 2 minutes. Stir in flour and curry powder. Stir to a smooth paste. Add both milks and cook 5 minutes, stirring every minute. Blend in remaining ingredients. Mix well and cook 6 minutes, stirring after 2 minutes. Serve with plain boiled rice and toasted coconut. (Mango chutney optional).

Vegetables

Beets with Orange Sauce

Very little water is required to cook vegetables in a microwave oven. Consequently, they retain their colour and vitamin content.

Vegetables will cook faster and more easily if their dish is covered.

Add variety and flavour to your vegetables. Try basil with tomatoes, celery seed with beetroot and cabbage. Use paprika to garnish cauliflower or corn. Grated cheese is great on broccoli, asparagus and Brussels sprouts. Add the cheese just before serving and heat for only 15 seconds.

Frozen vegetables may be cooked in the microwave oven by placing the plastic bag on a dish and piercing several holes into the bag.

Canned vegetables can be heated by draining off some of the liquid from the tin and pouring the rest into a casserole. Cover the dish and heat for 2 minutes for each cup of vegetables. Always season after heating.

CABBAGE

TIME: 7 MINUTES (HIGH)   SERVES 4-6

500 g shredded cabbage, washed and
    drained
2 cloves garlic, chopped finely
1 tablespoon butter
2 large peeled tomatoes, roughly
    chopped
salt

Place all ingredients in a small casserole dish or an oven bag lightly tied with string or an elastic band. Prick bag once or twice near opening. Cook 7 minutes, turning once during cooking.

LEAF SPINACH

TIME: 7 MINUTES (HIGH)   SERVES 4

500 g spinach leaves, no stalks, washed
    and drained
1 tablespoon butter
1 small onion, finely chopped
¼ teaspoon nutmeg
60 g peanuts, roughly chopped

Place spinach, butter, onion, and nutmeg into an oven bag. Fasten with an elastic band. Prick twice near opening. Cook 7 minutes, turning once during cooking. Top with roughly chopped peanuts.

CAULIFLOWER AU GRATIN

TIME: 9 MINUTES (HIGH)   SERVES 4-6

2 tablespoons butter
500 g cauliflower florets
¼ teaspoon garlic salt
pepper
2 large peeled tomatoes sliced
1 cup cheese sauce (see sauce section)
chopped parsley
paprika

Cook butter in casserole 20 seconds to melt. Add cauliflower, garlic salt, pepper and cook covered for 6 minutes. Top with sliced tomatoes, cheese sauce and parsley. Cook 3 minutes. Dust lightly with paprika before serving.

PARSLEY POTATO BALLS

TIME: 12 MINUTES (HIGH)   SERVES 4-6

750 g potatoes
water
2 tablespoons butter
parsley, finely cut
salt

Cut potatoes into balls using a melon baller. Place into casserole with water. Cook covered for 12 minutes, stirring twice during cooking. Cook butter 20 seconds to melt. Add parsley and salt. Pour over drained potatoes. Stir to coat.
Note: Chopped mint may be used in place of parsley.

BEETS WITH ORANGE SAUCE

TIME: 17 MINUTES (HIGH)   SERVES 4

4 precooked beetroots (page 63)
2 tablespoons brown sugar
1 cup orange juice
2 tablespoons tarragon vinegar
1 tablespoon butter
1 tablespoon cornflour

Use a melon baller and scoop out balls of beetroot from cooked beets. Combine sugar, juice, vinegar, butter and cornflour in a bowl. Cook 3 minutes, stir and cook until boiling. Add beets, cook 2 minutes and serve.

HONEY GLAZED CARROTS

TIME: 10½ MINUTES (HIGH)	SERVES 4

500 g carrots, cut into strips

Place in casserole dish with 1 tablespoon water. Cook covered 7-8 minutes, stir twice during cooking, drain.

HONEY SAUCE
1 tablespoon butter
2 tablespoons honey
2 tablespoons vinegar
2 tablespoons orange juice
salt
2 teaspoons cornflour

Combine all ingredients, place into glass dish and cook 1 minute. Stir after 30 seconds. Pour over carrots, cook 2 minutes to reheat.

VEGETABLE MEDLEY

TIME: 20 MINUTES (HIGH)	SERVES 4-6

250 g cauliflower florets
125 g carrots, sliced crosswise
250 g Chinese cabbage, sliced
125 g sliced mushrooms
1 small can asparagus spears
2 slices ham, diced
chopped parsley

Place cauliflower and carrots into a casserole dish. Add 2 tablespoons water and cook covered for 6 minutes. Place carrots and cauliflower into a larger casserole, cover with cabbage, mushrooms and asparagus spears. Spoon sauce over, top with ham and parsley. Cook covered 6 minutes.

SAUCE
2 tablespoons butter
2 tablespoons flour
1 cup chicken stock
2 cups milk

Cook butter to melt 20 seconds. Stir in flour and cook 2 minutes. Stir in stock and milk. Cook 6 minutes until thick and boiling. Stir during cooking.

CARROTS WITH MARSALA

TIME: 8 MINUTES (HIGH)	SERVES 4-6

500 g carrots, sliced crosswise
1 onion, chopped finely
1 tablespoon brown sugar
75 ml Marsala
1 tablespoon butter

Combine all ingredients and place into casserole dish just large enough to hold all ingredients. Cook 7-8 minutes, stirring twice during cooking.

SCALLOPED SWEET POTATOES

TIME: 15 MINUTES (HIGH)	SERVES 6

750 g orange sweet potatoes, sliced thinly
2 rashers of bacon, diced and precooked
2 tablespoons flour
1 teaspoon salt
½ cup shallots, finely cut
2 cups milk
1 cup tasty cheese, grated nutmeg and paprika
parsley, chopped

Combine all ingredients in a greased casserole dish. Cover and cook 15 minutes, stirring every 4 minutes. Sprinkle with extra nutmeg, paprika and chopped parsley.

BRAISED RED CABBAGE

TIME: 12 MINUTES (HIGH)   SERVES 6

½ head sliced red cabbage
2 tablespoons butter
2 green apples, peeled and sliced
1 small onion, chopped
½ teaspoon salt
¼ teaspoon pepper
2 cloves
1 bay leaf
2 tablespoons tarragon vinegar
1 cup dry red wine
1-2 tablespoons brown sugar

Combine all ingredients in a casserole. Cook covered 12 minutes, stirring every 4 minutes.

VEGETABLE KEBABS

TIME: 6 MINUTES (HIGH)   SERVES 4

Spear a variety of vegetables onto bamboo satay sticks, for example, cherry tomatoes, mushroom caps, chunks of red and green capsicums, canned mini corn, small onions, and zucchini. Cook 6 minutes, turning every minute and basting with a mixture of melted butter and lemon juice.

JACKET POTATOES

TIME: 11 MINUTES (HIGH)   SERVES 4

4 even-sized potatoes, unpeeled
peanut oil
4 tablespoons sour cream
2 rashers bacon, diced, precooked
chopped chives
herb butter

Prick potatoes, brush with oil and wrap in plastic food wrap. Place in a circle on oven tray and cook 5 minutes. Turn over and cook a further 6 minutes. Remove wrap and cut a cross on top of each potato. Squeeze firmly so that the centre will pop up. Top with herb butter, sour cream, bacon and chives.

ZUCCHINI SPECIAL

TIME: 8 MINUTES (HIGH)   SERVES 4

500 g unpeeled zucchini, sliced
1 tablespoon butter
onion or garlic salt
1 teaspoon fresh chopped dill
1 large peeled tomato, seeds removed,
   roughly chopped

Place all ingredients into a small casserole. Cover and cook 8 minutes.

FRESH BROCCOLI HOLLANDAISE

TIME 8 MINUTES (HIGH)   SERVES 4

500 g fresh broccoli
1 tablespoon water
2 tablespoons butter
onion salt

Cut broccoli into even lengths, remove skin from stalk and split ends with a knife. Place into a covered casserole dish or oven bag, with water, butter and onion salt. Cook 8 minutes. Arrange onto serving dish and mask with Hollandaise sauce. (See sauce section.)

COOKING CHART FOR FRESH VEGETABLES

Item	Quantity	Directions	Suggested Cooking Time in Minutes
Asparagus	500 g	¼ cup water, ⅓ teaspoon salt in covered casserole	5-6
Beans	750 g	⅓ cup water, ¼ teaspoon salt in covered casserole	12-14
Beetroot	4 whole medium	Wrap each bulb in plastic wrap	12-16
Broccoli	1 small bunch	cut away stalk, ½ cup water, 1 teaspoon salt in covered casserole	8-11
Brussels sprouts	500 g		
Cabbage	750 g chopped	3 tablespoons water, ⅓ teaspoon salt in covered casserole	8-10
Carrots	4 medium sliced	¼ cup water, ⅓ teaspoon salt in covered casserole	8-10
Cauliflower	750 g	⅓ cup water, ⅕ teaspoon salt in covered casserole	10-12
Celery	6 cups	¼ cup water, ⅓ teaspoon salt in covered casserole	10-12
Corn	3 ears	remove silk, leave husk on and tie with elastic band	12
Corn kernels	3 cups	⅓ cup water, ⅓ teaspoon salt in covered casserole	8
Eggplant	1 medium	¼ cup water, ⅓ teaspoon salt in covered casserole	8-10
Onion	2 large (cut in quarters)	½ cup water, ⅓ teaspoon salt in covered casserole	8-10
Parsnips	4 medium (cut in quarters)	½ cup water, ⅓ teaspoon salt in covered casserole	8-10
Green Peas	500 g	⅓ cup water, ⅓ teaspoon salt in covered casserole	6-8
Spinach	500 g	Put in casserole with water to cling to leaves, ⅓ teaspoon salt and cover	6-7
Potatoes	1 medium 2 medium 3 medium 4 medium 5 medium 6 medium 7 medium 8 medium	Scrub potatoes, and place on paper towel leaving a 2.5 cm space between potatoes. Note: Prick potatoes before placing in oven	5 7 9 12 14 16 20 22
Potatoes	4 medium (thinly sliced)	2 tablespoons butter in casserole, sprinkle with salt and dot with butter. Cover	11
Sweet Potatoes	2 medium	Place on paper towel, leaving 2.5 cm space between potatoes	7-8

COOKING CHART FOR FROZEN VEGETABLES

Item (315 g package)	Directions for All Vegetables	Suggested Cooking Time in Minutes
Asparagus		5–6
Broccoli		8–9
Beans, cut		8–12
Beans, French cut		7–8
Beans, Lima		8–9
Cauliflower	Cook in pouch that has been pierced	5–6
Corn, kernels		4–5
Corn on the cob		5–6
Mixed vegetables		6–7
Okra		6–7
Peas and carrots		5–6
Spinach		4–5

Rice

Vegetable Rice

Rice can be cooked in a microwave oven in eight minutes, two-thirds of the normal cooking time. Brown rice takes only 15 minutes to cook in a microwave oven—a considerable time saving.

Always wash rice before cooking it. The best way to do that is to place it in a colander and let cold water run over it.

When cooking rice remember that rice triples in bulk during cooking time. Allow 50 g or ¼ cup of uncooked rice per person, and let it cook in 500 ml or 2½ cups of water.

Always cook rice covered with a fitted glass lid or a plastic wrap, and allow rice to stand covered for 5 minutes before serving. The rice will finish cooking while covered. It is best to use a large casserole dish, to prevent spill-overs during cooking.

The method of cooking rice in the following recipes is the absorption method. Should you prefer the grains to be separate, the rice may be washed in hot water after cooking and allowed to drain.

If you cook more rice than needed at the one time, remember that rice can be stored in an airtight container in a refrigerator for one week, or it can be frozen for longer periods. You can then serve it cold, covered in a vinaigrette dressing, or coated with a thinned down mayonnaise.

To defrost frozen rice, allow 2 minutes in the microwave oven using the *Defrost Cycle*.

RICE

TIME: 8 MINUTES (HIGH)	SERVES 4

1 cup washed rice
pinch of onion salt
nob of butter
2 cups boiling water

Place rice into 1 litre casserole dish, add salt, butter and pour over boiling water. Cover. Cook 8 minutes. Allow to stand 10 minutes before serving.

FRIED RICE

TIME: 11 MINUTES (HIGH)	SERVES 4

3 rashers bacon
30 g fresh mushrooms
1 small onion
2 shallots
30 g shelled prawns
2 eggs
3 cups cold cooked rice, cooked
   with 1 chicken cube (method above)
1 tablespoon dark soy sauce

Dice bacon, mushrooms, onions, shallots and prawns. Place bacon onto glass dish, cover with white kitchen paper and cook 3 minutes. Remove from dish, add onion, mushrooms and cook 2 minutes. Fold lightly beaten eggs into rice, and add to dish. Cook 2 minutes, then stir, add bacon, soy sauce and stir mixture again. Cook 2 minutes. Stir in shallots and prawns. Cook 2 minutes to reheat. Season.

SAFFRON RICE

TIME: 11 MINUTES (HIGH)	SERVES 4

15 g butter
1 small onion, chopped
¼ teaspoon powdered saffron
   or turmeric
1 cup washed rice
30 g currants or sultanas
2 cups boiling chicken stock
   (can use stock cube)
30 g almond slivers, toasted

Place butter into 1 litre casserole dish and cook 15 seconds. Add onion, saffron and cook 3 minutes. Add rice, currants and boiling stock. Cook covered 8 minutes. Allow to stand for 10 minutes. Sprinkle with almonds before serving.

GINGER SAFFRON RICE

TIME: 8 MINUTES (HIGH)	SERVES 4

1 cup washed rice
pinch of salt
2 tablespoons diced red capsicum or
   crystallised ginger
½ teaspoon powdered saffron
nob of butter
2 cups boiling water

Place rice into a 1 litre casserole, add salt, capsicum or ginger, saffron, butter and boiling water. Cook for 8 minutes. Allow to stand for 10 minutes before serving. Can be moulded and turned out onto a serving plate.

Ginger Saffron rice

TOMATO RICE

TIME: 8 MINUTES (HIGH)	SERVES 4

1 cup washed rice
½ teaspoon sugar
pinch oregano
pinch onion salt
nob of butter
1 cup tomato juice
1 cup chicken stock
chopped parsley

Place rice into a 1 litre casserole dish, add sugar, spices, butter and boiling juice and stock. Cook covered 8 minutes. Allow to stand for 10 minutes. Sprinkle with chopped parsley. Serve with chicken dishes or casseroles.

RICE PILAFF

TIME: 14 MINUTES (HIGH)	SERVES 4

60 g butter
1 small onion, chopped finely
1 cup long grain rice, washed
2 cups boiling chicken stock
salt and pepper

Place 30 g of butter and the onion into a casserole dish. Cook 3 minutes, stir in rice. Cook a further 3 minutes. Add stock, seasonings, cover with a lid and cook 8 minutes. Mix in remaining butter, allow to stand 5 minutes before serving.

Variations of rice pilaff

MUSHROOM PILAFF
125 g sliced fresh mushrooms can be added to the rice and cooked as above.

VEGETABLE PILAFF
TIME: 14 MINUTES
30 g cooked peas
30 g diced capsicum
30 g diced tomato
60 g grated cheese

Prepare rice pilaff as above. After cooking for 8 minutes, fold all ingredients into rice with remaining butter and allow to stand 5 minutes before serving to heat through.

PAELLA

TIME: 13 MINUTES (HIGH)	SERVES 4-6

3 tablespoons oil
1 cup onion, sliced
1 clove garlic, minced
1 cup uncooked rice, washed
2 cups chicken stock, boiling
1½ teaspoons salt
¼ teaspoon saffron
⅛ teaspoon pepper
1 can (125 g) prawns, drained
1½ cups cooked chicken, 2 cm cubes
6 mussels, in the shell
1 cup peas
½ cup stuffed olives, sliced

Heat oil in a 2 litre casserole for 3 minutes. Add onion, garlic and heat a further 2 minutes. Add rice, chicken stock, salt, saffron, pepper and cook for 3 minutes. Stir. Fold in prawns, chicken, mussels and peas and cook a further 5 minutes, stirring after 2½ minutes. Add olives. Remove from oven and allow to stand for 10 minutes before serving.
Note: Keep casserole covered while cooking.

Paella

VEGETARIAN RICE

TIME: 9 MINUTES (HIGH)	SERVES 4–6

2 tablespoons butter
3 cups cooked rice
1 carrot, diced
1 clove garlic, finely minced
1 slice of ginger, finely minced
2 large mushrooms, finely minced
1 onion
2 tablespoons parsley, chopped
½ red capsicum
½ green capsicum
1 cup corn kernels
1 cup peas
salt and pepper
hard-boiled eggs

Dice all vegetables to the size of the corn. Wash and drain. Place butter into a 2 litre casserole. Cook 15 seconds. Add all the vegetables and cook covered 4 minutes. Fold in rice and add salt, pepper, garlic and ginger and parsley. Cook 5 minutes, covered. Garnish with diced hard-boiled eggs.

Desserts and Cakes

Frozen Grasshopper Torte

Cakes baked in a microwave oven require careful watching because of the rapid cooking process.

White or yellow cakes do not brown but, as most cakes are frosted, this should present no problem.

Use greaseproof paper to line the bottom of your baking dish if the cake is to be removed before serving.

Do not use waxed paper under cakes as the wax may melt.

For best results, grease the baking dish first, then line it with greaseproof paper and grease again.

Remember that overcooking toughens a cake.

Cook cakes until a wooden skewer inserted into the centre of the cake comes out clean.

When the cake is cold wrap it in plastic food wrap and it will remain fresh for one week.

GRASSHOPPER TORTE

| TIME: 3 MINUTES (HIGH) | SERVES 8 |

⅓ cup butter
1 package chocolate flavoured plain
   biscuits, crumbed
4 cups white marshmallows, diced
¾ cup milk
¼ cup green creme de menthe
2 tablespoons white creme de cacao
2 teaspoons gelatine
2 tablespoons cold water
1 cup stiffly beaten cream

Place butter in glass bowl and cook for 45 seconds. Stir in biscuit crumbs. Put half the mixture into a 23 cm round glass dish. Chill. Place marshmallows and milk into a large bowl. Cook 1½ - 2 minutes to melt marshmallows. Stir in creme de menthe and creme de cacao. Blend gelatine and water in small bowl. Heat 15 seconds on high. Blend into mixture. Cool. Fold in whipped cream. Pour into crumb-lined dish. Top with remaining crumbs. Chill until firm. Cut into wedges and pipe with whipped cream.

PINEAPPLE MERINGUE PIE

| TIME: 13 MINUTES (HIGH) | SERVES 8 |

PASTRY
125 g butter
⅓ cup sugar
2 cups plain flour, sifted
3 drops vanilla
2 teaspoons water
1 egg yolk

Rub butter into sugar and flour. Add vanilla, water and egg yolk. Knead lightly and let rest 15 minutes. Roll out pastry and line a 23 cm pie plate. Prick well and cook for 4 minutes. Allow to cool.

FILLING
500 g can pineapple, crushed
1 egg yolk
2 tablespoons custard powder
1 tablespoon arrowroot
¼ cup orange juice

Place pineapple into a casserole dish and cook 4 minutes until boiling. Beat egg yolk, add custard powder, arrowroot and orange juice. Mix into hot pineapple and cook for 2 minutes. Cool and spoon into pastry case.

MERINGUE
3 egg whites
½ cup castor sugar

Beat egg whites, adding sugar, 1 tablespoon at a time, until soft peaks form. Pipe or spread over pineapple filling and cook to set for 2-3 minutes. Place under grill for a few minutes if a light golden colour is required.

SAVARIN

| TIME: 6 MINUTES (HIGH) | SERVES 8 |

60 g butter
105 g castor sugar
3 eggs
125 g self-raising flour
2 tablespoons milk or cream

Beat softened butter and sugar to a cream. Add eggs, one at a time. Add flour, all at once. Fold in milk or cream. Grease and line base of micro-ring dish. Grease again. Pour in mixture and cook 5-6 minutes. Turn out on a cooking rack.

SYRUP
225 ml water
250 g sugar
5 tablespoons Grand Marnier

Boil water and sugar to form a syrup. Add Grand Marnier. Spoon warm syrup over cake until all is absorbed. Place onto a serving platter. Fill centre with fresh fruit salad. Decorate with whipped cream and extra fruit.

BABA AU RHUM

TIME: 11 MINUTES (HIGH)	SERVES 8

FRUIT
1 tablespoon raisins
1 tablespoon currants   } Combine
1 tablespoon sultanas
1 tablespoon rum

60 g butter
105 g castor sugar
3 eggs
125 g self-raising flour
2 tablespoons milk

Cream butter and sugar. Add eggs, one at a time. Add flour all at once and fold in milk and fruit. Place batter into a greased and lined glass Baba mould. Cook 5-6 minutes. Turn out on a serving platter.

SYRUP
½ cup sugar
1 cinnamon stick
1 cup syrup from tinned apricots
2 tablespoons lemon juice
4 tablespoons rum

Combine sugar, cinnamon stick and syrup together and cook 5 minutes. Add lemon juice and rum. Cool.

Spoon syrup over Baba. Serve decorated with whipped cream, apricots and glace cherries.

APPLE CRUMBLE

TIME: 9 MINUTES (HIGH)	SERVES 6-8

6 cooking apples, peeled and sliced
½ cup water
½ cup sugar
½ teaspoon cinnamon
60 g soft butter
¼ cup plain flour
½ cup coconut
½ cup brown sugar

Place apples, water, sugar and cinnamon into a 1 litre casserole dish, cover and cook 5 minutes. Rub butter into flour, coconut, brown sugar and sprinkle over apples. Top with extra cinnamon and cook 3-4 minutes. Serve with custard sauce.

PINEAPPLE GINGER CAKE

TIME: 10 MINUTES (HIGH)	SERVES 8

60 g butter
⅓ cup brown sugar
6 small slices of canned pineapple
6 maraschino cherries

Cream butter and brown sugar together and spread into the bottom of a baking dish. Place pineapple rings into mixture with a cherry in the centre of each ring.

CAKE
80 g butter
½ cup white sugar
1 egg
½ cup golden syrup
⅓ cup milk
1½ cups plain flour
1 teaspoon bicarbonate of soda
1 teaspoon ground ginger
1 teaspoon ground cinnamon
pinch salt

Cream together butter and sugar, add egg, golden syrup and milk. Sift dry ingredients together. Blend all into a creamy mixture. Spread over pineapple slices. Cook uncovered for 10 minutes.

Note: Other fruits may be used: sliced mangoes, peaches or apricots.

Pineapple Coconut Cake page 80

BAKED BREAD AND BUTTER CUSTARD

| TIME: 62 MINUTES (DEFROST) | SERVES 6 |

30 g butter
2 cups milk
5 eggs
¼ cup raw sugar
1 teaspoon vanilla
4 slices white bread, crusts removed,
   then buttered
nutmeg
2 tablespoons sultanas

Place butter into milk and heat for 2 minutes. Beat eggs, sugar and vanilla, add milk and butter mixture. Sprinkle buttered bread lightly with nutmeg, cut into cubes, and place into a greased baking ring with sultanas. Pour custard over bread and cook uncovered 60 minutes on the *Defrost Cycle*.

RICE CUSTARD

| TIME: 22 MINUTES |

Note: 1 cup of precooked rice can be used in place of the buttered bread.

QUEEN PUDDING

| TIME: 63 MINUTES (DEFROST & HIGH) | SERVES 6 |

4 slices of buttered, stale plain cake
5 eggs
2 tablespoons sugar
2 cups warm milk
vanilla
strawberry jam

Cut cake into cubes. Place into a well-buttered baking ring. Beat eggs, sugar and vanilla, add warm milk. Pour over cake cubes and cook 60 minutes on the *Defrost Cycle*. Spread top of custard with strawberry jam. Top with piped meringue (see recipe from Pineapple Meringue Pie) and cook 2-3 minutes. Sprinkle with sugar lightly coloured with a few drops of pink food colouring.

CARAMEL TART

| TIME: 8 MINUTES (HIGH) | SERVES 8 |

1 precooked pastry case — see recipe from Pineapple Meringue Pie

2 tablespoons butter
1 cup brown sugar
4 egg yolks
3 drops vanilla
pinch salt
2 tablespoons plain flour
2 cups milk

Beat butter and sugar until fluffy. Beat in egg yolks. Add vanilla, salt, fold in sifted flour, stir in milk. Cook 4-5 minutes, stirring every minute until mixture thickens. Spoon into pastry case. Top with meringue and cook 2-3 minutes on high.
Note: For meringue, see recipe from Pineapple Meringue Pie.

CHOCOLATE SOUFFLE

| TIME: 7½ MINUTES (DEFROST) | SERVES 6 |

6 teaspoons gelatine
¾ cup sugar
3 eggs, separated
1 cup milk
60 g melted cooking chocolate (chop or
   grate chocolate, and cook ¾-1
   minute to melt)
1 cup whipped cream

In a large bowl combine gelatine with ½ cup sugar. Stir in egg yolks and beat in the milk. Heat on the *Defrost Cycle* for 6½-7½ minutes or until gelatine dissolves, stirring occasionally. Stir in chocolate and chill, stirring occasionally until mixture mounds slightly. Beat egg whites until soft peaks form, gradually add remaining sugar and beat until stiff. Fold in the chocolate mixture with whipped cream. Pour into a souffle dish with a collar. Chill. To serve, garnish with extra whipped cream and almond slivers.

Chocolate Soufflé

STRAWBERRY PAVLOVA

TIME: 4 MINUTES (MEDIUM)   SERVES 8

4 egg whites
1 cup castor sugar
½ teaspoon vanilla
¾ teaspoon white vinegar
3 teaspoons butter, melted
cornflour

Beat egg whites until soft peaks form. Add ⅓ cup sugar, beat until dissolved. Gradually add remaining sugar. When dissolved, add vanilla and vinegar, beating 1 minute. Grease a 23 cm pie plate with melted butter, dust well with cornflour and shake off any excess. Spoon meringue into pie plate leaving a higher outside edge than in the centre. Cook 3 minutes. Place under preheated grill until pale golden if desired.

FILLING
½ cup strawberry jam
2 teaspoons brandy
1 punnet strawberries, hulled, washed and dried
whipped cream

Heat jam to melting point, 1 minute on high, then sieve. Blend in brandy. Cut strawberries in halves, coat lightly with jam. Spread top of pavlova with cream, pile strawberries on top of cream. Pipe rosettes of cream around outside edge.

STRAWBERRY CREAM DESSERT

TIME: 7 MINUTES (DEFROST)   SERVES 6-8

2 punnets ripe red strawberries
4 eggs, separated
1 tablespoon gelatine
8 tablespoons sugar
1 carton whipped cream

Wash and hull strawberries. Place 1½ punnets into a blender and puree. Blend puree, egg yolks, gelatine and sugar. Place into a glass bowl and cook on the *Defrost Cycle* 7 minutes until gelatine dissolves, stirring constantly. Chill until slightly set. Beat cream to form stiff peaks. Fold into strawberry puree and beaten egg whites. Pour into individual glass sweet dishes to set. Decorate with whipped cream and remaining strawberries.

PEACHES FLAMBE

TIME: 5½ MINUTES (HIGH)   SERVES 4

30 g butter
1 can drained peach halves
2 tablespoons Grand Marnier
30 g sugar
3 extra tablespoons Grand Marnier for flaming

Heat butter in glass serving dish for 1-2 minutes. Add peach halves and Grand Marnier. Sprinkle with sugar and cook 3 minutes. Heat extra Grand Marnier in glass jug for 25 seconds, flame and pour over peaches. Serve with vanilla ice cream.

LEMON MERINGUE PIE

TIME: 7 MINUTES (HIGH)   SERVES 8

1 precooked pastry case — see recipe from Pineapple Meringue Pie
1 quantity of whipped meringue — see recipe from Pineapple Meringue Pie

FILLING
½ cup cornflour
½ cup sugar
¾ cup water
⅓ cup lemon juice
⅓ cup butter
3 egg yolks
grated rind of 1 lemon

Combine cornflour, sugar, water, juice of lemon and butter in a casserole dish and cook 2 minutes, stir and cook a further 2 minutes. Cool. Beat in yolks and lemon rind. Place in pastry case. Top with meringue, cook 2-3 minutes. Cool.

BAKED HONEY PEARS

TIME: 8 MINUTES (HIGH)   SERVES 4

4 firm pears
4 tablespoons chopped dates
2 tablespoons chopped
   walnuts   } Combine
3 tablespoons honey
¼ teaspoon cinnamon

Peel pears. Cut off caps 2.5 cm from top. Core each pear without cutting right through. Remove seeds. Fill centres with date mixture, replace caps. Arrange in a circle on a glass plate and cook 6-8 minutes. Pears can be served whole: remove cap and top with whipped cream, or cut in half, served with a rosette of whipped cream.

APPLE TEA CAKE

TIME: 6 MINUTES (HIGH)   9 MINUTES (MEDIUM)

60 g butter
¾ cup sugar
vanilla
1 egg
¾ cup milk
1½ cups plain flour
2 teaspoons baking powder
½ teaspoon salt
1 green apple, peeled, cored and sliced
   thinly
2 teaspoons brown sugar
2 teaspoons cinnamon

Cream butter, sugar and vanilla until light and fluffy. Beat in egg and fold in milk and sifted dry ingredients except the apple, brown sugar and cinnamon. Prepare the micro-baking dish, grease it first, then line it with greaseproof paper and grease it again. Place in thinly sliced apples and lightly dust with mixture of brown sugar and cinnamon. Pour batter on top of apples. Cook 6 minutes on high or 9 minutes on medium.

PINEAPPLE COCONUT CAKE

TIME: 6 MINUTES (HIGH)   9 MINUTES MEDIUM

60 g butter
¾ cup sugar
vanilla
1 egg
½ cup milk
1 cup drained crushed pineapple
½ cup coconut
1½ cups plain flour
1 teaspoon baking powder
½ teaspoon salt

Cream butter, sugar and vanilla until light and fluffy. Beat in egg and fold in milk, crushed pineapple, coconut and sifted dry ingredients. Prepare micro-baking dish. Pour mixture into dish and cook 6 minutes on high or 9 minutes on medium.

GINGER PUFF SPONGE

TIME: 2½ MINUTES (HIGH)

2 eggs
60 g sugar
1 teaspoon golden syrup
30 g cornflour
30 g plain flour
2 level teaspoons ground ginger
1 level teaspoon cinnamon
1 level teaspoon cocoa
¼ level teaspoon bi-carb of soda
½ level teaspoon cream of tartar

Beat eggs until thick and creamy, gradually adding sugar, beating until dissolved. Add golden syrup and beat until well mixed. Fold in sifted dry ingredients. Place into a well-greased micro-baking ring and cook for 2½ minutes, turning every minute. When cold, split and fill with cream.

80

MERINGUE-TOPPED CHOCOLATE CHEESE CAKE

TIME: 9 MINUTES (HIGH & DEFROST)

BASE
1 cup biscuit crumbs
½ cup melted margarine (to melt
   margarine put in oven ¾ - 1 minute)

Combine ingredients and press evenly into a 20 cm pyrex pie plate. Chill until firm.

FILLING
375 g cream cheese (to soften
   cheese, cut up and place in oven on
   the *Defrost Cycle* for 1 minute)
2 eggs
½ cup castor sugar
1 teaspoon vanilla
60 g melted chocolate (to melt
   chocolate, cut up and place in oven
   and cook 1 minute)

Beat cream cheese using an electric mixer until smooth. Add eggs one at a time. Add sugar, vanilla, and beat until creamy smooth. Pour into crumb crust. Swirl in melted chocolate to give a marble effect. Cook 3 minutes.

TOPPING
2 egg whites
5 tablespoons castor sugar
⅓ cup coconut
2 teaspoons cornflour

Whip egg whites until stiff, using an electric beater, gradually adding sugar, beating to dissolve. Fold in coconut (can be lightly toasted if desired) and cornflour. Pipe onto cheese cake and cook 3 minutes. Serve cold.

BANANA CAKE

TIME: 10½ MINUTES (MEDIUM)

60 g butter, melted
¼ cup milk
1 egg, beaten
½ cup mashed banana
½ cup brown sugar
1 cup self-raising flour
½ cup chopped nuts

Combine butter, milk, egg, banana, and brown sugar in a basin. Mix well. Fold in flour and nuts. Pour into a greased and lined round 21 cm pyrex souffle dish. Sprinkle with topping. Cook on medium 10½ - 11½ minutes. Let stand 5 minutes before turning out.

TOPPING:
¼ cup brown sugar
¼ cup chopped nuts
1 tablespoon plain flour   ⎫
2 tablespoons coconut   ⎬ Combine
pinch cinnamon   ⎭
15 g softened butter

MARBLE CAKE

TIME: 6 MINUTES (HIGH)

60 g butter
¾ cup sugar
vanilla
1 egg
¾ cup milk
1½ cups plain flour
2 teaspoons baking powder
½ teaspoon salt

Cream butter, sugar and vanilla until light and fluffy. Beat in egg, fold in milk and sifted dry ingredients alternately. Divide the mixture into 3 separate bowls:
   1) Leave one plain.
   2) Add a few drops of red food colouring to the
      second one.
   3) Add 2 tablespoons cocoa, pinch of bi-carb and 1
      tablespoon milk to the third.
Drop into greased, lined micro-baking ring in alternate colours. Lightly mix with a metal skewer to blend colours. Cook 6 minutes on high.

CARROT CAKE

TIME: 9 MINUTES (HIGH & MEDIUM)

½ cup butter or margarine
½ cup firmly packed brown sugar
1 egg
1 cup firmly packed fresh grated carrot
1 dessertspoon crystallised ginger
½ cup seeded raisins
½ cup sultanas
1½ cups double sifted plain flour
1 teaspoon baking powder
½ teaspoon soda
½ teaspoon cinnamon
½ teaspoon nutmeg
¾ cup milk

Cream butter or margarine and brown sugar. Beat in egg until well blended. Stir in carrots, ginger, raisins and sultanas. Sift together flour, baking powder, soda, cinnamon and nutmeg. Stir into the mixture with milk. Blend well. Turn into a well greased micro-ring dish and cook in oven 6 minutes high and 3 minutes medium. Serve cold with lemon frosting or hot with lemon sauce.

FROSTING:
250 g icing sugar mixture
90 g cream cheese
3 tablespoons butter
1 teaspoon vanilla
1 teaspoon sherry

Beat all ingredients until fluffy — spread over cake. Decorate with mandarin quarters or small marzipan carrots.

ORANGE TEA RING

TIME: 6 MINUTES (HIGH)   9 MINUTES (MEDIUM)

60 g butter
¾ cup sugar
vanilla
1 egg
3 tablespoons orange juice
3 tablespoons milk
2 teaspoons orange rind, grated
1½ cups plain flour
2 teaspoons baking powder
½ teaspoon salt

Cream butter, sugar and vanilla until light and fluffy. Beat in egg and fold in orange juice, milk, orange rind and dry ingredients alternately. Drop into a greased, lined and greased micro-baking ring. Cook for 6 minutes. Cool and top with orange frosting.

DATE LOAF

TIME: 6 MINUTES (HIGH)   9 MINUTES (MEDIUM)

2 tablespoons butter or margarine
½ cup raw sugar
1 egg
⅔ cup milk
½ cup dates
½ cup walnuts, chopped
1½ cups self-raising flour
pinch salt
½ teaspoon cinnamon
½ teaspoon ginger
1 teaspoon mixed spice

Beat butter and sugar to a cream. Add well-beaten egg. Add milk gradually. Add chopped dates and nuts. Stir in lightly the sifted flour, salt, and spices. Spoon mixture into prepared micro-baking dish. Cook 6 minutes on high or 9 minutes on medium.

BLACK FOREST CHERRY CAKE

TIME: 12 MINUTES (HIGH)

1 packet chocolate cake mix

FILLING
1 can black cherries, stoned
⅓ cup Kirsch
2 tablespoons arrowroot
3 tablespoons cherry syrup
300 ml cream
grated dark chocolate
red cherries

Make as directed on packet. Grease and line a microwave baking ring. Pour cake mix into prepared dish. Cook in oven 5½-6 minutes. Turn onto a cake cooler and cover before cake is cold.

Place cherries, 2 tablespoons of Kirsch and syrup from cherries into a bowl to cover. Cook 4 minutes or until boiling. Blend arrowroot with 3 tablespoons syrup. Stir into cherry mixture, cook 2 minutes and allow to cool. Split cake into 3 layers. Spread cherry mixture over base, top with second layer. Whip cream with remaining Kirsch. Spread half over second layer, top with third piece of cake. Spread top and outside edges lightly with cream. Mark top into serves. Dust top and sides with grated chocolate. Pipe a rosette of cream on edge of each marked portion and top with a whole red cherry.

Black Forest Cherry Cake

Sauces and Jams

Parsley Sauce

Sauces are very quick and easy to make
in a microwave oven.

Be sure to stir frequently when making sauces.
You can leave a wooden spoon in the bowl in
the oven to make this a simple operation.

Always use a large glass container for sauce
preparation to prevent boiling over.

When thickening sauces remember that
arrowroot makes a more transparent sauce than
one thickened with cornflour.

BASIC WHITE SAUCE I (BECHAMEL)

TIME: 10½ MINUTES (HIGH)

1 small onion, peeled
6 whole cloves
600 ml milk
1 bay leaf
60 g butter
60 g plain flour
salt and pepper

Stud onion with cloves. Pour milk into a glass jug, add onion and bay leaf. Cook on high for 4½ minutes to heat and infuse flavours.
Place butter into a glass jug or casserole and cook 1 minute to melt. Add flour and stir with wooden spoon. Cook 1 minute.
Stir in milk to blend. Cook for 4 minutes, stirring after 2 minutes. Remove onion and bay leaf.
Season with salt and pepper.

CHEESE SAUCE I

60 g grated tasty cheese
1 egg yolk, beaten

Add 2 tablespoons of Basic White Sauce I to egg yolk and beat quickly. Return to remainder of sauce, along with cheese. Reheat for 2 minutes if necessary.
Do not allow to boil.

Use with seafood or vegetables.

PARSLEY SAUCE

2 tablespoons parsley, chopped

Fold 2 tablespoons of parsley into Basic White Sauce I.

Use with seafood, vegetables, or corned meats.

ONION SAUCE

60 g onion, diced

Melt butter in Basic White Sauce I recipe. Add onion and cook 3-4 minutes before adding the flour.
Add milk and cook as above.

Use with roast mutton, corned beef, or corned ox tongue.

EGG SAUCE

2 hard-boiled eggs

Dice eggs finely. Fold into Basic White Sauce I. A little finely cut parsley may also be added.

MUSHROOM SAUCE (Made from Veloute Sauce, page 92)

125 g sliced button mushrooms
   (canned mushrooms can be sliced
   and used if a mild flavour is required)
1 egg yolk, beaten
4 tablespoons fresh cream

Melt butter in a jug or casserole. Add mushrooms and cook for 1 minute. Blend in flour and cook a further 1 minute. Blend in warm stock (veal or chicken) and cook 4 minutes to thicken.
Stir after 2 minutes. Combine egg yolk and cream.
Add 2 tablespoons of sauce, blend well and fold into remaining sauce. Season with salt and pepper.
Use with steak, veal or chicken.

CHASSEUR SAUCE TIME: 13 MINUTES (HIGH)

30 g butter
1 shallot, cut finely
60 g mushrooms, sliced
50 ml dry white wine
125 g tomatoes, chopped, deseeded
300 ml demi glace sauce
parsley, chopped

Cook butter in a casserole for 1 minute. Add shallots and cook 2 minutes. Add mushrooms and cook covered 2 minutes. Drain off butter. Add wine and cook 2-3 minutes until boiling and reduced to half. Add tomatoes, demi-glace sauce and cook 5 minutes. Add parsley, salt and pepper.

Use with steaks, chicken, barbecued food or lamb.

BASIC WHITE SAUCE II TIME: 4 MINUTES (HIGH)

2 tablespoons butter
2 tablespoons flour
½ teaspoon salt
little white pepper
250 ml milk

Place butter in a glass bowl. Cook for 45 seconds or until melted. Stir in flour, salt and pepper. Add milk and cook approximately 3 minutes until boiling, stirring from time to time. Makes 1 cup.
Note: Use a wooden spoon when stirring.

CHEESE SAUCE II

Ingredients are the same as above except that you add ¼ teaspoon dry mustard with the flour. After sauce has cooked, stir in ½ to 1 cup shredded cheese until melted.

HOLLANDAISE SAUCE TIME: 1 MINUTE 45 SECONDS (HIGH)

⅓ cup butter
2 tablespoons lemon juice
2 egg yolks
¼ teaspoon salt

Place butter into a small bowl, heat for 45 seconds. Stir in lemon juice and egg yolks, beat with whisk until well mixed. Cook 60 seconds, whisking every 15 seconds. Stir in salt halfway through.

BASIC BROWN SAUCE TIME: 12 MINUTES (HIGH)

30 g butter
60 g carrot, diced
60 g onion, diced
30 g celery, diced
45 g pre-browned flour
1 tablespoon tomato paste
1 bayleaf
600 ml brown stock

Place butter into a casserole, cook 1 minute to melt. Add carrots, onion and celery, cook 4 minutes. Blend in flour and cook 1 minute. Add tomato paste, bay leaf, blend in stock and cook 3 minutes, stir well and cook another 3 minutes. If slower cooking is required, cook sauce on the *Defrost Cycle* for 15-20 minutes, stirring from time to time. Strain.

Use with roast meats or as a base for other sauces.

DEMI GLACE SAUCE TIME: 6 MINUTES (HIGH)

300 ml brown sauce
250 ml brown stock
50 ml Madeira

Combine ingredients in a jug. Cook 4-6 minutes, stirring twice during cooking time.

AURORA SAUCE

1 tablespoon tomato puree

Add puree to sauce supreme to enrich flavour and colour.

Use with chicken, poached eggs or pasta dishes.

CURRY SAUCE TIME: 11 MINUTES (HIGH)

30 g butter
1 clove garlic, chopped
60 g chopped onion
1 tablespoon curry powder
30 g plain flour
2 teaspoons tomato paste
450 ml chicken stock or fish stock for seafood
60 g apple, chopped
1 tablespoon fruit chutney
1 tablespoon sultanas
1 tablespoon chopped almonds
salt and pepper

Cook butter in casserole 1 minute to melt. Add garlic, onion and curry powder. Cook 3 minutes, blend in flour and cook 1 minute. Add tomato paste and stock, blend with wooden spoon. Add remaining ingredients and cook 4-6 minutes, stirring after 2 minutes.

Serve with seafood, poultry, hard-boiled eggs or vegetables.

MINT SAUCE TIME: 9 MINUTES (HIGH)

250 g sugar
60 g arrowroot
dash salt
500 ml warm water
2-3 drops green food colouring
1 teaspoon finely chopped mint
2 drops peppermint essence

Combine sugar, arrowroot and salt in a 4-cup glass measure. Stir well, add water. Cook for 6 minutes, stirring after first 2 minutes and then after every minute. Bring to boil. Add food colouring, chopped mint, and essence. Heat for 30 seconds.

APPLE SAUCE TIME: 12 MINUTES (HIGH)

500 g cooking apples
3 tablespoons water
30 g butter
30 g sugar
¼ teaspoon cinnamon or nutmeg

Peel, core and slice apples. Place into a casserole with sugar, butter and water. Cook covered for 12 minutes or until a puree is formed. Stir twice during cooking. Strain, stir in nutmeg or cinnamon.

Serve with roast pork or poultry.

TOMATO SAUCE TIME: 14 MINUTES (HIGH)

1 medium onion chopped
1 large clove garlic
500 g fresh tomatoes, peeled and chopped
2 bay leaves
2 teaspoons sugar
½ teaspoon dry basil
2 tablespoons tomato paste
1 tablespoon butter
1 cup stock
salt
pepper

Melt butter in pyrex dish 30 seconds. Add onion, garlic. Cook 4 minutes on high. Add remaining ingredients. Cook on high 10 minutes, remove bay leaves. Puree mixture.

VELOUTE SAUCE
—This is a basic sauce, a little darker in colour. Chicken, fish or veal stock is used in place of milk.

TIME: 11 MINUTES (HIGH)

60 g butter
60 g plain flour
600 ml stock (suitable for sauce required)
salt and pepper

Place stock into a glass jug and cook on high for 4 minutes. Place butter into a jug or casserole dish, cook 1 minute to melt. Stir in flour with wooden spoon. (A wooden spoon may be left in sauce during cooking for ease of stirring.) Cook 2 minutes. Blend in stock. Continue cooking for 4 minutes, stirring well after 2 minutes. Add seasonings.

SUPREME SAUCE (Made from Veloute Sauce) TIME: 8 MINUTES (HIGH)

30 g mushroom trimmings
1 egg yolk
squeeze lemon juice
75 ml fresh cream
600 ml warm chicken sauce

Using basic ingredients, cook butter to melt and add mushrooms and cook 2 minutes. Blend in flour, cook a further 1 minute. Blend in stock and cook 4 minutes. Stir after 2 minutes. Add seasonings, stir well and strain. Blend cream and egg yolk. Add 2 tablespoons sauce, mix well and return to remaining sauce, add lemon juice.

Use with hot boiled chicken or as a basic sauce for pastry or bread cases.

PORT WINE SAUCE TIME: 6 MINUTES (HIGH)

300 ml demi glace sauce
3 tablespoons port wine
30 g butter

Cook sauce in jug for 3-4 minutes. Add port wine and cook 2 minutes. Blend in the butter.

Use with roast or barbecued meats.

CUSTARD SAUCE I TIME: 6 MINUTES (HIGH & DEFROST)

375 ml milk
3 tablespoons sugar
2 tablespoons custard powder
2 egg yolks
1 teaspoon vanilla

Combine custard powder and sugar with milk. Heat 4 minutes on high, until sauce thickens, stirring twice. With a wire whisk quickly beat in the egg yolks, heat for 1-2 minutes on the *Defrost Cycle*, then flavour with vanilla.

CUSTARD SAUCE II TIME: 6½ MINUTES (HIGH)

300 ml milk
1 tablespoon custard powder
30 g castor sugar

Blend custard powder with a little milk. Place remaining milk into a glass jug. Cook 4½ minutes. Blend in custard powder and cook 2 minutes.
Mix sugar in to dissolve.

CHOCOLATE SAUCE TIME: 5 MINUTES (HIGH)

300 ml milk
75 g sugar
1 teaspoon butter
15 g cocoa
15 g cornflour

Blend cornflour, cocoa with 3 tablespoons milk. Place remaining milk into a jug and cook 3 minutes to boil. Blend in cornflour mixture and cook 2 minutes. Blend in sugar and butter.

PLUM JAM TIME: 32½ MINUTES (HIGH)

1 kg plums
crystal sugar
juice 3 medium lemons

Cut plums into small pieces removing stones. Place into a dish and cook approximately 20 minutes until a pulp is formed. Allow 1 cup sugar for every cup pulp. Warm sugar in oven for 30 seconds. Add sugar and lemon juice to fruit pulp. Cook approximately 12 minutes until a gel is formed, stirring occasionally. Pour into sterilized jars. Cool slightly, label, date and seal.

STRAWBERRY JAM TIME: 20 MINUTES (HIGH)

500 g strawberries
1½ cups crystal sugar
juice small lemon

Chop strawberries roughly, place into oven with sugar and lemon juice. Cook approximately 20 minutes, stirring occasionally. Remove, pour into sterilized jars, label, date and seal.

APPLE AND PEAR JAM TIME: 32 MINUTES (HIGH)

500 g apples, peeled and sliced
500 g pears, peeled and sliced
sugar
juice 3 lemons

Place peeled and sliced apples and pears into a dish and cook approximately 20 minutes until a pulp is formed. Allow 1 cup sugar for every 1 cup pulp. Warm sugar in oven for 30 seconds. Add sugar and lemon juice to fruit pulp. Cook approximately 12 minutes, stirring occasionally until a gel is formed. Pour into sterilized jars. Cool, label, date and seal.

LEMON BUTTER TIME: 8 MINUTES (DEFROST)

Rind and juice of 1 large lemon
60 g butter
⅓ cup sugar
2 60 g eggs
pinch salt

Combine all ingredients in a medium bowl. Cook covered on the *Defrost Cycle* for 6-8 minutes, stirring occasionally until thickened. Store in hot, sterile jars, in a cool, dry place.

ORANGE MARMALADE TIME: 50 MINUTES (HIGH)

700 g oranges
1 lemon
3 cups sugar, heated

Wash and dry fruit. Cut in half, squeeze out the juice. Cut peel into very thin strips. Place peel into a large pyrex bowl. Make up the juice to 3 cups with water. Pour over fruit. Cover and cook on high 20 minutes. Add sugar to cooked peel. Cook on high for 30 minutes or until jam is at setting consistency. Bottle whilst hot.

INDEX

Poultry

Apricot Chicken Casserole 40
Braised Lemon Chicken 38
Chicken in Red Wine 40
Chicken Satay 44
Chilli Chicken 42
Crumbed Chicken Drumsticks 41
Gourmet Chicken 40
Mexican Chicken 38
Red Roast Chicken 42
Roast Chicken 44
Roast Orange Duck 44
Roast Turkey 47
Spanish Chicken 38
Sweet and Sour Chicken 42

Seafood

Baked Orange Fish 52
Coquilles St. Jacques 54
Curried Prawns 54
Fillets of Flounder with Pernod Sauce 49
Fresh Trout with Asparagus Sauce 54
Garlic Prawns 49
Oysters Kilpatrick 49
Oysters Mornay 49
Salmon Ring 49
Salmon Stuffed Mushrooms 50
Scallops in Oyster Sauce 52
Smoked Salmon Quiche 50
Whole Fish with Black Bean Sauce 50
Whole Fish with Chinese Pickle Sauce 52

Vegetables

Beets with Orange Sauce 58
Braised Red Cabbage 62
Cabbage 58
Carrots with Marsala 60
Cauliflower au Gratin 58
Cooking Chart for Vegetables 63
Fresh Broccoli Hollandaise 62
Honey Glazed Carrots 60
Jacket Potatoes 62
Leaf Spinach 58
Parsley Potato Balls 58
Scalloped Sweet Potatoes 60
Vegetable Kebabs 62
Vegetable Medley 60
Zucchini Special 62

Rice

Fried Rice 67
Ginger Saffron Rice 67
Mushroom Pilaff 68
Paella 68
Rice 67
Rice Pilaff 68
Saffron Rice 67
Tomato Rice 68
Vegetable Pilaff 68
Vegetarian Rice 70